Enc <!-- barcode: MW01059187 -->

ENCOUNTERS WITH JESUS

FRANK BARKER

WITH MAUREEN RANK

While this book is designed for the reader's personal enjoyment and profit, it is also intended for group study. A Leader's Guide with reproducible response sheets is available from your local bookstore or from the publisher.

VICTOR BOOKS®

A DIVISION OF SCRIPTURE PRESS PUBLICATIONS INC.
USA CANADA ENGLAND

Unless otherwise noted, Scripture quotations are from the *Holy
Bible, New International Version*, © 1973, 1978, 1984, International Bible
Society. Used by permission of Zondervan Bible Publishers. Quota-
tions marked TLB are from *The Living Bible*, © 1971, Tyndale House
Publishers, Wheaton, IL 60189. Used by permission. Other quota-
tions from the *King James Version* (KJV).

Recommended Dewey Decimal Classification: 232.903
Suggested Subject Heading: CHARACTER AND PERSONALITY OF JESUS

Library of Congress Catalog Card Number: 88-62856
ISBN: 0-89693-620-1

CONTENTS

CHAPTER ONE

Jesus and the Thirsty Woman

God goes after the lost. I know, because of the trouble He took to pursue me. During my pre-Christian days, I lived in immorality and rebellion without any attention to God. But one night I fell asleep at the wheel and ran my car off the road. I came out of the mishap unscathed, but my car stopped directly in front of a huge sign that read, "THE WAGES OF SIN IS DEATH!" How's that for taking special pains to get my attention? Jesus sought, and still seeks, the lost.

Early in his public ministry, Jesus left Jerusalem, heading north to Galilee. The Scripture makes a point of emphasizing that He *had* to go through the province of Samaria. Why? Because a woman waited there who needed desperately to come to God, so God sent His Son to find her.

Now [Jesus] had to go through Samaria. So He came to a town in Samaria called Sychar, near the plot of ground Jacob had given to his son Joseph. Jacob's well was there, and Jesus, tired as He was from the journey, sat down by the well. It was about the sixth hour.

When a Samaritan woman came to draw water, Jesus said to her, "Will you give Me a drink?" (His disciples had gone into the town to buy food.)

The Samaritan woman said to Him, "You are a Jew and I am a Samaritan woman. How can you ask me for a drink?" (For Jews do not associate with Samaritans.)

Jesus answered her, "If you knew the gift of God and who it is that asks you for a drink, you would have asked Him and He would have given you living water."

. . . .

The woman said, "Sir, give me this water so that I won't get thirsty and have to keep coming here to draw water."

He told her, "Go, call your husband and come back."

"I have no husband," she replied.

Jesus said to her, "You are right when you say you have no husband. The fact is, you have had five husbands, and the man you now have is not your husband. What you have just said is quite true."

"Sir," the woman said, "I can see that you are a prophet. Our fathers worshiped on this mountain, but you Jews claim that the place where we must worship is in Jerusalem."

Jesus declared, "Believe Me, Woman, a time is coming when you will worship the Father neither on this mountain nor in Jerusalem. . . . God is spirit, and His worshipers must worship in spirit and in truth."

The woman said, "I know that Messiah," (called

Christ) "is coming. When He comes, He will explain everything to us."

Then Jesus declared, "I who speak to you am He."

. . . .

Many of the Samaritans from that town believed in Him because of the woman's testimony, "He told me everything I ever did." So when the Samaritans came to Him, they urged Him to stay with them, and He stayed two days. And because of His words many more became believers (John 4:4-10, 15-21, 24-26, 39-41).

A map of Palestine shows that the shortest distance from Jerusalem to Jesus' home country cut through Samaria. But no self-respecting Jew would have taken that route. Better to spend extra hours on the road than to risk having to associate with the hated Samaritans.

Samaritans were religious half-breeds, offspring of mixed marriages between Israelites and the idol-worshiping Assyrians. They claimed to worship God, but set up their own temple on Mt. Gerizim, instead of honoring the temple at Jerusalem. Jews hated Samaritans, but the hatred was reciprocated. A hundred years before Christ, the Jews destroyed the Samaritan's temple, so a Samaritan band scattered bones on the porch of the temple at Jerusalem.[1]

In Christ's day, Jews traveling through Samaria were often attacked. Once when Jesus sought lodging while on a trip through Samaria, He was refused, simply because Jerusalem was His destination. (His Jewish disciples showed their contempt for their Samaritan neighbors by suggesting Jesus call down fire from heaven to consume the Samaritans for their lack of hospitality! Jesus, of course, refused.)

But ignoring custom, Jesus sought out a hated Samaritan. To make matters worse, this Samaritan was also female.

The Jews thought it scandalous for an educated man to speak to a woman in a public place. Some extremists even objected to men talking to their own wives on the street, and considered talking with any other woman in public as justifiable grounds for divorce. Rabbis instructed, "It would be better that the Articles of the Law be burned than that their contents be revealed to a woman publicly."[2] Yet Christ initiated a conversation with her. God the Seeker was at work. In this interaction, He shows us that He can meet our needs, help us forsake our deceptions, then transform us into colaborers with Him in His harvest of souls.

Jesus Offers Living Water—but Only to the Thirsty

Jesus told the Samaritan woman He could provide water that would satisfy her thirst forever. She replied, "Sir, give me this water so that I won't get thirsty...." She could have chosen other replies. She could have said, "Thanks, but I'm not thirsty." Or, "I don't need any help; I can get all the water I need by myself." If she had not admitted her need, she never would have been a candidate to receive all Christ had to give.

When the Pharisees sniped at Jesus for befriending tax collectors, He responded, "It is not the healthy who need a doctor, but the sick. I have not come to call the righteous, but sinners to repentance" (Luke 5:31-32). Jesus came to help those in need. He seeks out the needy, not the well; the poverty-stricken, not the satisfied; the hungry, not the full. Luke says of Christ, "[He] healed those who needed healing" (Luke 9:11).

In our world, the epitomy of success is a need-free life. We want to be financially free, pain free, stress free, and hassle free. In other words, our goal is to be God-free, our lives safely under our own control. And isn't this the temptation that has faced humanity since the time of Adam and Eve? "Eat . . .," the serpent hisses to us, "and you will be as gods" (Gen. 3:4, KJV). Deities are self-sufficient. They owe no one, need no one, can be hurt by no one, depend on no one. They stand alone, solitary and invincible.

But the truth is, we can never be need-free, nor do we want to be. The Lord firmly rebuked the church in Laodicea because they said, " 'I am rich; I have acquired wealth and *do not need a thing*.' But you do not realize that you are wretched, pitiful, poor, blind and naked" (Rev. 3:17, emphasis author's). This spirit of self-sufficiency is what the Lord spoke against when He told the disciples, "It is easier for a camel to go through the eye of a needle than for a rich man to enter the kingdom of God" (Mark 10:25). Jesus wasn't saying riches in themselves are evil. But having wealth may make it harder for us to see how needy we actually are. One wealthy man in Oklahoma likes to say, "You know the Golden Rule? He who has the gold makes the rules!" Perhaps that's why not many rich, or wise, or influential, or status-born come to Christ. God intends that our boast be in Him, but if we think we deserve His favor, or worse yet, we've done the work ourselves, we'll depend on ourselves, and not on Him.

But to those willing to admit their need, Christ becomes a need-meeter. He promised this woman living water to quench her thirst, and He supplied it. He healed the sick, offered friendship to the lonely, gave rest to the overburdened, and forgave the guilty. But in each case, He was free to work, because the recipient of His help admitted a need. Of course, He is also able to humble the proud, and bring the hard-hearted to repentance.

Do we need Christ's help? Are we willing to be vulnerable to Him and receive it? This Samaritan woman was, and found the Lord true to His word.

Intellectual Arguments Don't Cover Sin

When the woman asked for living water, she responded to what she understood of God's offer of life. But instead of beginning a theological treatise on salvation, Jesus said, "Go, call your husband and come back." I'm sure the woman's face fell, and a slight blush crept onto her cheeks as she answered a little too quickly and a little too loudly, "I have no husband." What she said was technically correct, but as many of us do when we're cornered, we pick out one fact from the ten relevant ones, and tell only what puts us in the best light. She didn't lie . . . exactly, but her answer didn't communicate the truth, either. "You are right when you say you have no husband," Jesus said. "The fact is, you have had five husbands, and the man you now have is not your husband. What you have just said is quite true."

Trapped in a lie. How embarrassed she must have been. But at this moment, the woman had a chance to reveal herself to Jesus as she was, and confess her sin. Everyone who does business with God must face just such a moment, because God will only forgive those who admit they've done something wrong. Later, the Apostle John would write, "If we claim to be without sin, we deceive ourselves and the truth is not in us" (1 John 1:8). You can't be healed from a disease you deny you have.

Jesus gave the Samaritan woman a chance to get it over with quickly. He spelled out her sin, so she could have simply agreed with him, and identified her need for mercy from God. Had she done so, forgiveness would have been immediately forthcoming. But instead of agreeing that her behavior had been sinful, she tried to distract Jesus with a diversion into intellectual debate that would take the heat off her need.

"Sir," the woman replied, "I can see that You are a prophet. Our fathers worshiped on this mountain, but you Jews claim that the place where we must worship is in Jerusalem" (5:19-20).

We've got to give her credit for some quick thinking. Without missing a beat, she tried distracting Jesus with flattery, and then diverting Him into debating a popular and heated question of the day about where worship must take place. Jesus probably smiled to Himself when He heard her question. She was to be the first of many who would try this ploy when they realized receiving His life might cost them something. Belief in the Gospel necessitates a willingness to change our lives. When we receive Christ, we embrace a Saviour, but we also bow before a Lord. Even today, those who want no-fault salvation quickly hide behind intellectual difficulties to keep from revealing their own need. Sometimes the plea that "I don't understand" actually means, "I don't want to change."

Recently, a friend and I spent two hours in mental gymnastics with a man who was investigating the Gospel. He jumped from this question to that, and though we tried to answer, he seemed to move no closer toward a commitment to Christ. Later, I found out the man was living in adultery, and also had a reputation for highly questionable business practices. I wondered then if his reluctances about the Gospel were actually intellectual, or moral ones instead. Perhaps his questions served to justify keeping God at arm's length, so nothing in his life would have to change. I thought then of a saying I'd heard: "Why is it most intellectuals don't believe the Gospel? For the same reason most nonintellectuals don't believe the Gospel!" True belief demands repentance, and repentance demands a willingness to live under God's control instead of our own.

Don't misunderstand. The Lord doesn't rudely wave away all questions as devious ploys to avoid meeting Christ. Jesus didn't deliver a sarcastic lecture on the woman's need to confess her immortality. He talked about where to worship, but He drew her gently back to the real issue of her sin. "A time is coming and has now come when the true worshipers will worship the Father in spirit and in truth" (5:23). And for emphasis, He repeats the message. "God is spirit, and His worshipers must worship in spirit and in truth" (5:24). A genuine relationship with God demanded that she tell the truth. Instead she'd tried to lie about her sinfulness. But her sin would have to be confronted if living water was to be hers. "He who conceals his sins does not prosper, but whoever confesses and renounces them finds mercy" (Prov. 28:13). Sinfulness is no problem to God, because He can forgive without limit, but sinfulness that hides behind intellectual sparring is a great problem.

Is there a sin you're trying to cover? Are you so busy chasing after an analysis of your behavior that you aren't simply calling it sin, and asking Christ to forgive you? God won't allow us to cover sin with intellectual arguments. He's fully able to forgive and deliver from any sin, so He sees no need to cover it. Jesus gave the woman no psychological analysis of her sin; He rather gave her opportunity to call it what it was, so she could be forgiven. "If we confess our sins, He is faithful and just and will forgive us our sins and purify us from all unrighteousness" (1 John 1:9).

The Samaritan woman must have responded to His requirement, because the main impression she took back to others from their conversation was "He told me everything I ever did." It wasn't the heavy teaching, or the theological bantering that left its greatest mark on her.

Instead, her forgiven past became the foundation for her new life.

When God Finds Us, We Want to Help Him Seek Others

The Messiah sought and found a sinful woman of Samaria and satisfied her thirst from the fountain of living water. Then she ran back to her village and told others there about Him. They, in turn, came to hear Him and asked Him to stay two days, and many of them believed Him to be the Saviour of the world.

It's helpful to remember that these Samaritans who invited Jesus and His disciples to stay with them were inviting hated Jews into their town. This miraculous truce in the war between the Jews and Samaritans, and the coming of salvation that followed it, began because one woman came to faith, and then ran to tell those she knew. When God finds us, we want to help Him find lost ones, as well.

After spending one day with Jesus, Andrew believed Him to be the Messiah. And the first thing Andrew did as a new believer was to find his brother Peter and bring him to the Lord. Jesus called Philip to follow Him, and as Philip responded, he took time out to invite Nathanael to come too. Matthew, the tax collector, trusted Christ and then put on a large banquet for other tax collectors, so they could know Him too.

Have you allowed Jesus to give you an assignment in His harvest field? Perhaps you haven't because you fear what the assignment will be, but you need not fear. The task He will assign will fit you perfectly, since He created and gifted you to serve. He called David the shepherd boy to become the shepherd of God's chosen people. He asked fishermen to join Him in fishing for the souls of men and women. He challenged some to leave their homes; others, He directed to stay at home and tell of what He'd done. He has no blanket assignment for all; instead, He tailors your place in the harvest to the abilities and gifts and desires He placed in you.

Some years ago, a woman began attending our church at the invitation of her seven-year-old stepson. She was as attractive as a debutante, but she was illiterate. She'd grown up in foster homes and, during years of being shuffled from this school to that, never learned to read or write. Like the woman at the well, she'd always faked her way by telling lies like, "I forgot my glasses," so others wouldn't know her embarrassing secret.

But then she met Christ at a Billy Graham crusade, and she so badly wanted others to know about Him, she admitted her need and enrolled in reading lessons. But even then, she decided not to wait until she read proficiently to share the good news of Christ. So she took a Gospel tract to those in her apartment complex with this introduction. She'd say, "I'm your neighbor. I'm a new Christian, and I'm so excited about what's happened to me, I want you to know about it. I have a little book that explains it, but I'm just now learning to read. If you will help me read it, I believe we can get through it together." They'd read the book, and she led many to Christ. She even brought her reading teacher to the Lord. This woman's task in God's harvest fit her strengths—and her weaknesses—perfectly, and so it will be for you.

The Samaritan woman could have listed dozens of reasons why she shouldn't tell those in her village about Christ. She had a reputation for immorality, so she might have feared ridicule if others found out she'd "gotten religion." And she was an outcast, indicated by the fact that she came alone to the well to draw water. (According to the custom of the day, drawing the day's supply of water provided a social gathering for the village women as they met around the well, so all came at the same time.

And the water-fetching was done in the cool of the morning, not in the heat of noonday when this woman came to the well, underscoring her "outsider" position.) She could have used her lack of social status as a reason to keep the news of the Messiah to herself. But Christ's life in us is like putting a whole box of detergent into an agitating washing machine. The suds invariably overflow.

When this woman pointed those she knew to Christ, her whole village was changed. The outcast became an insider, as her neighbors found the Saviour.

We belong to God who came to us in our need. He removed our need to hide our sin when He forgave and cleansed us. Then He lifted us up to work alongside Him in His mission to touch a needy world.

In the pages ahead, we'll look together at eleven other encounters between individuals and the Lord. In them, you'll meet people like your neighbors, and your family, and even yourself. Some are devout; others, immoral. Some shine with great faith; some thrash in a bog of doubt. The righteous as well as the rascals are here. Jesus praised some, prodded others, and exhorted and encouraged them all with a view to developing their trust in God.

NOTES

1. William Coleman, *Today's Handbook of Bible Times and Customs* (Minneapolis, Minnesota: Bethany House Publishers, 1984), p. 250.

2. Gien Karssen, *Her Name Is Woman* (Colorado Springs, Colorado: NavPress, 1975), p. 175.

CHAPTER TWO

Jesus and the Workaholic

LINDBERGH FLIES NEW YORK TO LONDON IN LESS THAN 34 HOURS! Back in 1927, headlines bannered it as the technological achievement of the century. Last year, the United States government unveiled an experimental jet capable of making the same trip in under two hours. Two hours! If all of life has speeded up at the same rate our air travel has, we're now living 1,700% faster than we were sixty years ago.

Life at the end of this twentieth century has pitted the human race against the rat race—and it looks as if the rats are winning. If God wants to speak to us, He will have to leave a message on our answering machine. We're too tied up in our workaholic busyness to wait for His call.

But is workaholism a malady created by the Computer Age? The Bible says it isn't. Nearly 2,000 years ago, workaholism plagued Martha of Bethany, one of Jesus' closest supporters. The tenth chapter of Luke records the Lord's attempt to help His workaholic friend. Her story may be simple, but it is rich with applications for those of us who work desperately to make ourselves worth something, instead of living at peace and letting Christ tell us who we are.

> As Jesus and His disciples were on their way, He came to a village where a woman named Martha opened her home to Him. She had a sister called Mary, who sat at the Lord's feet listening to what He said.
> But Martha was distracted by all the preparations that had to be made. She came to Him and asked, "Lord, don't You care that my sister has left me to do the work by myself? Tell her to help me!"
> "Martha, Martha," the Lord answered, "you are worried and upset about many things, but only one thing is needed. Mary has chosen what is better, and it will not be taken away from her" (Luke 10:38-42).

Workaholism Can Result from Overusing a Spiritual Gift

When we Bible teachers expound on this story of these two sisters, we're always quick to drive home the Lord's words as a clear and uncompromising rebuke to Martha. And well we should. But we need to begin by scoring a point in Martha's favor. She was using her spiritual gift. She employed it enthusiastically, aggressively, and persistently.

She could have done otherwise. Maybe Jesus and His disciples stopped in unannounced. Martha could have refused them. She could have heard their knock, and hissed to her brother Lazarus, "Don't answer it! It's almost time for dinner, and I've only got enough lamb chops for the three of us. Besides, the place is a mess." Or she might have invited them in, and begun making excuses. "We'd love to have you spend the night, but we're getting new furnishings for the guest room and they haven't arrived yet." Some of us come up with a thousand excuses for not using the gifts God has given us. "When the kids get older," we explain, or "When we have more money," or "When I don't have so many responsibilities" or "When our church gets a pastor I can work with better than this one. . . ."

Not so with Martha. God gave her a heart and ability to extend hospitality to others. When Jesus needed food and lodging, she welcomed Him, even though using her gift would cost time and money and just plain hard work.

And Martha was no fair-weather friend, only entertaining Christ to raise her prestige in the neighborhood. The Gospels tell of other times Jesus visited Bethany, and was most likely a guest in Martha's home. It appears He was always welcome there, even when He fell from favor with the Jewish establishment. Martha's continual identification with Him took courage and commitment. Charles Haddon Spurgeon said of her, "I think it is altogether wrong to treat Martha as if she had no love for the good things. Martha was a most estimable and earnest woman, a true believer, and an ardent follower of Jesus, whose joy it was to entertain Jesus at her house."[1]

So to all workaholics, a word of encouragement. You have some things to teach the rest of us about aggressiveness, initiative, and following through on commitments. We need to follow her example in grabbing our spiritual gift and running with it, even if using our gift means getting our elbows greasy, or our bank accounts depleted, or being with people we'd rather avoid. (Surely Jesus made a delightful guest, but with Him came an array of objectionable characters, including rough-and-tumble fishermen, a tax collector of questionable repute, and a political revolutionary.) Using our gifts can mean being pushed into uncomfortable situations with uncomfortable people. But Martha welcomed them. Jesus corrected

Martha for the wrongful use of her gift, but He certainly never rebuked her for using it. For that she's to be commended, as are all workaholics who use the gifts they've been given.

A Workaholic Loses Sight of Why She's Working

Imagine for a moment how it might have been. Jesus and His disciples relax in the living room of Martha's spacious home. Banter and questions and discussion bounce back and forth between them as they rehash the day. Mary sits quietly near her Lord, listening, and pondering His comments. There is a spirit of warmth and camaraderie that wraps around them all. All, of course, except Martha, who isn't a part of the group.

Crash! From the kitchen comes the sound of a clay pot smashing on the tile floor, followed by a groan loud enough to carry across three rooms.

"Martha, is everything all right?" Lazarus calls to his sister.

"Yes . . . of course. Everything's fine." Martha mouths the right response, but it comes out clipped and forced. "Just go on about your visiting, and don't pay any attention to me."

Lazarus turns to invite Jesus to finish His comments, and in a moment the room again buzzes with conversation.

Then from the side door, Martha pushes through the group, her arms piled so high with fresh bed linens that her nose barely grazes the top of the stack. "Excuse me, excuse me," she mutters loudly as she pushes between Peter and John, and then half-trips over Matthew's extended feet as she makes her way across the middle of the room to the door opposite.

Jesus stands and holds out His arms with a warm smile. "Martha, may I help?"

"Oh, no . . . no, of course not." She shakes her head and tries to return His smile. "I don't need help. You just go on with Your visit."

Jesus begins to speak again, but His words are cut short by a conversation in the hallway too loud to not overhear. "You didn't draw extra water as I told you." Martha's statement of facts sounds more like an accusation. Her servant girl attempts an explanation, but Martha shuts her off. "Do I have to do everything? Can't you see I have all these guests, and dinner to prepare? Is everyone else here totally helpless?" She finishes her tirade with a sigh and stomps off to the kitchen.

The Scripture says Martha's serving distracted her from Jesus. Not long before, she had welcomed *Him* into her home. He was her focus, the centering point of her attention. Now her attention had shifted away from Him. What distracted her from Christ? Worldly pleasures didn't. Others' criticisms couldn't. But this devout believer was pulled away from Christ by her own overdone service to Him.

Who insisted on a sumptuous meal, anyway? I doubt that it was Jesus, because He often was satisfied with the simplest fare. After His encounter with the woman at the well, He refused to eat at all. "My food," said Jesus, "is to do the will of Him who sent Me and to finish His work" (John 4:34). Jesus may not have needed the food, but perhaps Martha needed the sense of worth she gained from cooking it, even though she exhausted herself in the process.

The times I've overdone and made myself and everyone else miserable, it's been because I needed people's appreciation, or their pity, or their admiration too much. Like Martha, I was trying to prove I was worth something by my hard work.

Don't get me wrong. Working hard is not synonymous

with evil. The Book of Proverbs challenges us to show the same drive and hustle in our work that ants do. And if you've ever observed an ant farm, you know the "busy-as-a-bee" metaphor should have long ago been replaced by "ambitious as an ant." They keep at it long and hard and steadily. Jesus was a hard worker, as was the Apostle Paul, and nearly everyone since who has ever done a significant work for God. Working hard at the task Christ has given you is fine. But when service becomes a pain, or a means of personal gain, then the service needs to be curtailed for the sake of the higher good of resting in Christ's presence. God called you to be His beloved, not His beast of burden.

Pastor and author Alan Redpath was crippled in midlife by a brain hemorrhage. During his time of recovery he looked back over a life of aggressive service, including fourteen years preaching in London, another ten years at Moody Church in Chicago, and a successful pastorate in Edinburgh. But what he saw in retrospect amounted to years of distraction from Christ Himself.

"I thought I was so spiritual," Redpath reflected, "for I was working like any slave for the sake of God's dear Son seven days a week, fourteen hours a day, sometimes more. There was no time for home, no time for family, no time for anything but work. I had substituted work for the Lord Jesus, service for heart surrender, orthodoxy for obedience. I was so proud of my neat sermon outlines—three points, introduction, and conclusion, all points beginning with the same letter. I had substituted my knowledge of truth for my knowledge of God."[2]

Like Martha, Redpath missed the best by giving himself too completely to the good, and we're susceptible as well. Martha began with her focus on pleasing Jesus, but was distracted out of His presence by her own insistence on providing service He never expected.

Work Can Be a Defense against Intimacy

A tired, disheveled Martha could stand it no longer. She'd dropped all the hints she was going to. Enough was enough! With anger and disgust, she broke into the teaching session going on in the living room. "Lord, don't You care that my sister has left me to do the work by myself? Tell her to help me!"

Martha's complaint highlights another common mark of workaholism. "Lord, don't You care that my sister has left me to serve *alone?*" Workaholics are gold medalists at distancing themselves from those who care about them. When work comes before loving relationships, those relationships always suffer. If you're not convinced, ask the wife or husband of a compulsive overworker. To her credit, Martha, at least, was at home with her family and friends. Some workaholics never get that far. But her physical presence in the home didn't guarantee intimacy. While those close to her enjoyed each other, Martha was off communing with her work. And when she did come to the group, it apparently was to complain about those who weren't working, and to moan about Christ's lack of caring.

Some of us choose overwork for this very purpose. We're afraid of intimacy, either with Christ or with others, so our work becomes a convenient hiding place from the terror of being known, really known, by God and those we love. Work we can control. Work we can master. But close relationships are another thing. They demand vulnerability, openness, and sensitivity—qualities that threaten to assault our carefully constructed defenses against being hurt.

If we stay busy enough, we have a feeling that no one, not even God, will be able to see how small and insecure and uncertain we really feel. And if the work we do is good enough, perhaps God and His people will look at it and decide we're good enough too. Then we'll be worthy of love and belonging.

Indeed, both men and women succumb to the lure of workaholism. That makes it a genderless crime, but it certainly isn't a victimless one. The loved ones of workaholics always suffer. Martha treated her sister Mary rudely, embarrassing her before a roomful of their friends. And the accusation she leveled at Jesus ("Lord, don't You care . . .?") charged Him with unkindness and taking advantage. No wonder those who value service above relationships often wind up alone!

Workaholism's Most Debilitating Side Effect Is Joylessness
Jesus listened to Martha's outburst, and then observed, "Martha, you are worried and upset."

I wonder if Martha thought, *"Of course* I'm upset! *Naturally*, I'm troubled! I have a right to be anxious, since I've been left to do all the work. No one else seems to be worried, so I guess I'll have to worry for all of us."

Jesus challenged Martha's anxiety, because He knew a work done at God's instigation and in His strength is a work that exudes joy.

In our day, Mother Teresa and her Sisters of Charity serve the destitute and dying around the world with a passion and commitment even Martha would have envied. Many of the Sisters come from middle- to upper-class homes and are well educated. But they've left all this, renouncing all worldly goods to live like the destitute to whom they minister. If any of us have earned the right to feel pitiful and heavy-hearted, these Sisters surely have.

But British journalist Malcolm Muggeridge says this of them: "Their life is tough and austere by worldly standards, certainly; yet I never met such delightful, happy women, or such an atmosphere of joy as they create."[3]

Instead of self-pity, and complaining, and frustration, and weariness, they serve with joy—and rest. "Come to Me, all you who are weary and burdened, and I will give you rest," He invites, " . . . for . . . My burden is light" (Matt. 11:28-30). As soon as we feel overloaded in service to Christ, we can safely say this service we're supposed to be doing for Him has become something else. An ego trip, perhaps, or our attempt to earn His favor. But service to Him it isn't, because the burdens He gives rest lightly on us.

Balanced Living Comes Only by Choice

"Mary has chosen what is better," Christ told Martha. Mary didn't stumble onto the good; she deliberately chose it. Surely she felt pressure to do all Martha did, but she chose to give priority to developing her inner life. It will not happen otherwise. It requires planning, sacrificing, cutting things out, and resisting others' pressure. Intimacy with Jesus Christ doesn't ooze over us while we sleep, or crowd in on us while we give ourselves to work or television or play. It must be wooed in a deliberate, purposeful choice on our part.

But Mary did more than choose not to flutter about anxiously.

First, she chose to *sit*. When Christ came in the door, Mary chose to stop all other activities. In contrast, Martha opted for her anxious overpreparations, and let the best be replaced by the good. Many of our life choices rest not between good and evil, but rather between good and the best. Mary chose the best. She left good pursuits—pursuits the Scripture calls "serving"—for the higher call of being with Christ Himself. She chose to sit, trusting Christ would in turn help her with the serving that needed to be done.

Second, Mary chose to sit *at Jesus' feet*. She came to sit at the Lord's feet, and no one else's. Only His perspective would satisfy. And a second-hand account wasn't good enough, either. She determined to hear His words for herself.

Third, Mary *listened* to His teaching. She didn't situate herself at His feet, wait for everything to be quiet, and then launch into a two-hour monologue of all her thoughts and feelings and worries. She listened. She waited to hear His concerns and delights.

Spurgeon said: "You are not losing time when you are feeding the soul. When the man gets within him principles, vital, fervent energies, then when the season for work comes he will work with a power and a result which empty people can never attain, however busy they may be."[4]

Mary listened, and tuned in to the heartbeat of God. That's why later, as Christ faced the horror of His impending death, Mary could hear the prompting of God's Spirit, and bring her costliest perfume to anoint Him. Her tender act enraged the disciples. "What a waste," they railed. "Perfume costing a year's salary! The money could have been used so many better ways to further Christ's cause."

Christ rebuked them. During their times with Him, they sat at His feet, perhaps, but they hadn't learned to listen. Mary heard the promptings of God in a way the others didn't. And because she'd learned to listen, Christ said of her, "She has done a beautiful thing for Me" (John 12:7, TLB). To which of the disciples was such magnificent praise ever given? Her service to God wasn't marked by trouble and anxiety, grousing and complaining. Because she chose against pressing activity, and chose instead a quiet place at His feet, Mary's service became a beautiful thing to Christ. That's what Christian work was meant to be!

As you've read Martha's story, did you find it easy to substitute your own name for hers? If you did, then take courage as you remember that Jesus cared enough about this overworked servant to correct her. And remember that later when He came to raise her brother Lazarus from the dead, He detoured from His mission long enough to coax the reluctant Martha onto the solid rock of faith. Martha mattered to Him, as do you. He only asks that you leave your harried service to come away and listen to Him. In that place of quiet, you'll feel your burdens lighten as they are buoyed up by the joy of His pleasure in you.

NOTES

1. C.H. Spurgeon, *The Metropolitan Tabernacle Pulpit*, Vol. XVI (Pasadena, Texas: Pilgrim Publications, 1970), p. 230.

2. Ted Miller, Editor, *Meeting Life's Challenges* (New York, Harper and Row, 1983), pp. 88-89.

3. Malcolm Muggeridge, *Something Beautiful for God* (New York, Image Books, 1977), p. 37.

4. C.H. Spurgeon, p. 237.

CHAPTER THREE

Jesus and the Man Who Got Down to Specifics

I detest shopping. I would rather face a root canal than look for a new suit, would rather stare down a herd of stampeding buffalo than enter any mall in the world the day after Thanksgiving. My nightmares involve stores overrun by Serious Shoppers, dressed in their "Shop Till You Drop" T-shirts, eyes ablaze and nostrils flaring, charging through the aisles with all the vigor Teddy Roosevelt must have exuded as he headed up San Juan Hill. When I can't avoid shopping, I prefer to do it on a day when the stores are infiltrated by the window-shopping crowd who drift from counter to counter, trying on a squirt of cologne here, or a jacket there, but feel no pressure to buy anything.

Window-shopping has its pleasures, but we must be sure we don't let a "window-shopper's mentality" invade our prayer life. Catherine Marshall has some stern words to those who dabble in such low-risk praying:

"Window-shopping can be enjoyable—but there it ends. It costs nothing. We are just looking, have no intention of buying anything; so we bring nothing home to

show for the hours of browsing. Too many of our prayers—private and public—are just browsing amongst possible petitions, not down to cases at all. We expect nothing from our prayers except a euphoric feeling."[1] When
we window-shop in prayer, she warns, we're protecting
ourselves from the tension inherent in praying in faith.
On the way to His triumphal entry into Jerusalem,
Jesus met Bartimaeus, a blind beggar who called for help.
In their encounter, Jesus pulled Bartimaeus away from
generalized praying, into a faith that restored his sight.
Bartimaeus has much to teach us about prayers that move
God to act on our behalf.

> Then they came to Jericho. As Jesus and His disci-
> ples, together with a large crowd, were leaving the
> city, a blind man, Bartimaeus (that is, the Son of
> Timaeus) was sitting by the roadside begging. When
> he heard that it was Jesus of Nazareth, he began to
> shout, "Jesus, Son of David, have mercy on me!"
> Many rebuked him and told him to be quiet, but
> he shouted all the more, "Son of David, have mercy
> on me!"
> Jesus stopped and said, "Call him."
> So they called to the blind man, "Cheer up! On
> your feet! He's calling you." Throwing his cloak
> aside, he jumped to his feet and came to Jesus.
> "What do you want Me to do for you?" Jesus asked
> him.
> The blind man said, "Rabbi, I want to see."
> "Go," said Jesus, "your faith has healed you." Im-
> mediately he received his sight and followed Jesus
> along the road (Mark 10:46-52).

Many of us connect with Bartimaeus sitting by the side
of that road. He'd come to faith in Christ, this much was

obvious by his cry, "Son of David. . . ." This name wasn't loosely bandied about; Jews were well aware that the promised Messiah was to be born of David's lineage. Bartimaeus may have suffered physical blindness, but spiritually he saw clearly, for he believed Jesus was the coming Saviour. He didn't call to Jesus as teacher, or prophet, as others had done. He affirmed Jesus as the Son of David, the Redeemer for whom they had waited.

And Bartimaeus didn't hesitate to come when Christ called for him, even if it meant leaving his secure spot beside the road, and kicking away the cape that slowed him down. Again, many of us gladly respond when we hear the Master's call, even if it means leaving some hindrance that's tripping us up, be it a possession, or a relationship, or a position. We're aggressively willing to respond to His directives to us.

For us, Jesus' encounter with Bartimaeus holds an important lesson, because in their dialogue, Jesus gave this blind man a key that may dramatically change how often we see answers to our petitions. It can transform our drowsy browsing among our prayer requests to powerful prayer which focuses in and shakes loose a response from heaven.

Powerful Prayers Are Specific

"Son of David, have mercy on me," the blind man called out to Jesus. His request was certainly a scriptural one, since we serve a merciful God. But a general dusting of mercy wasn't what Bartimaeus needed. This blind beggar needed to see. Perhaps it seems foolish that he pleaded for mercy when his real need was sight. But when we stop and listen to our prayers, his undefined, general plea for help matches the cries that most of us make to God. "Lord, please do Your will in our church." "God, please bless my sister." "Pour out Your goodness upon our assembly." None of these requests is unscriptural, of course, but they don't do much to build faith.

Surely it occurred to Bartimaeus to ask for sight. I'm sure Bartimaeus knew Jesus had spent much of the last three years doing miracles, and the blind had more than once been joyful recipients of His healing touch. But the beggar cried only for a nebulous mercy. Why don't we just ask Christ for the concrete thing we need? I believe there are several reasons.

First, we could be bound by an unholy passivity we mistake for submission to the Lord's will. When God created the human race, he did not make us jellyfish. He created jellyfish to be jellyfish; He molded us in His image to walk and talk and interact with Him in a dynamic tension energized by love for each other. He rules and we gladly submit, of course, but because of His love and grace, our Sovereign has allowed us to be active participants in His work. We might not spell out our requests because we don't understand He wants us to be involved with Him.

Second, we may fear we're "using" God, or making Him into a celestial Santa Claus if our requests become too precise. But Jesus wanted Bartimaeus to define his particular need; the Lord took special pains to help the blind man hone his general cry for mercy into a more exact request for sight. If we refuse to pray well-defined requests, we may be like King Ahaz of Judah and find ourselves trying to be more spiritual than God.

The kingdom of Ahaz was under attack, and Ahaz and his people quaked with fear. So God came to Ahaz through the Prophet Isaiah, promising victory against these enemies. Then the Lord invited Ahaz to ask for a sign of reassurance that God would indeed do what He had said He would.

But Ahaz refused. "I'll not bother the Lord with anything like that" (Isa. 7:12, TLB).

Doesn't that sound pious? And terribly spiritual? Ahaz is obviously so full of faith he doesn't need a sign of assurance from God. However, God didn't agree and He soundly rebuked the king. Catherine Marshall says:

> The reason many of us retreat into vague general-
> ities when we pray is not because we think too highly
> of God, but because we think too little. If we pray
> for something definite and our request is not grant-
> ed, we fear to lose the little faith we had. So we fall
> back on the safe route of highly "spiritual" prayers—
> the kind that Jesus brushed aside as not true prayer
> at all, just self-deceptive "talking to ourselves."[2]

Third, we aren't definite because we fear we'll "ask amiss" or ask for something that's not good for us. Fear can paralyze us, and hold us off forever from concrete praying. Perhaps the "what-ifs" of fear bound Bartimaeus from being clear about his need. "What if God prefers to use me as a blind man, and I miss His best will by being healed?" "What if I get healed and can't find work? I don't have skills, and at least while I'm blind I can sup-port myself by begging. That income will be gone if I can see." "What if seeing makes me so self-sufficient I no longer need God? What if it results in my spiritual downfall?"

Some of us are more prone to the temptation to fear than others. Whenever "what-ifs" flood our minds, we can be sure our enemy is speaking; God isn't. Phooey on fears! If God willed Bartimaeus' sight to be restored, He would then provide all the former beggar would need to make a life of godliness and success in the world of the sighted. And if God's best good could be better served by Bartimaeus staying blind, wouldn't Jesus have gently explained this to our begging friend? Bartimaeus didn't need to make a judgment call for God. Nor did he need to fear asking wrongly, for the Lord's Word promises that if we ask amiss, we simply won't receive what we've asked for (James 4:3). If we make a mistake in what we ask for, God won't destroy us. He just won't give us what we ask for, and that's how we want it, anyway, isn't it?

Fourth, we sometimes don't restrict our prayers because we're not sure what we want. We may not know ourselves well, so instead of doing the work involved to decide what we want to see God do, we cop out like Bartimaeus tried to, and send to the Lord a generic plea for mercy. Faith teacher Russ Johnston has some timely advice for those of us learning to list our needs explicitly:

> You can't make a list of your needs without coming to some decisions about them. If you're miserable in your job, you still can't write something down to present to God until you've decided just what it is you really want to have happen. Do you want your own attitude changed about your present job? Do you want a new job? Are you seeing that even another job like the one you have won't satisfy you and that what you really want is to change fields?
>
> Making any such decision is hard work. It requires that you forsake those vague, restless feelings, leave behind all that griping-over-dinner to your wife about the boss, and move on out into what it is you really desire. But that's the decision that will activate your faith and bring it to life.[3]

Of course, there will always be times when we simply don't know what to pray for. Jesus will ask, "What do you want Me to do for you?" and we'll have to shrug our shoulders, and confess we don't know. In those times, there is one specific request we can always make. We can ask for wisdom, because the Lord instructs, "If any of you lacks wisdom, he should ask God, who gives generously to all without finding fault, and it will be given him" (James 1:5). And until His wisdom comes, we can always hold tight to the Lord's encouragement in Romans 8:26, "The Spirit helps us in our weakness. We do not know what we ought to pray, but the Spirit Himself intercedes for us with groans that words cannot express." His Spirit will intercede and shape our prayers aright until we come to understand what God would have us ask.

Are we like Bartimaeus, presenting petitions so general that we can't even tell when God answers? If God's mercy had crept in and settled like a thick fog over Bartimaeus, would the beggar have realized it as an answer to his prayer? Would the crowd have known God had moved? I think not. But when Bartimaeus told the Lord he needed sight, and received it, both he and the watchers around him exploded in praises to God. That's what effective prayer accomplishes!

Specific Requests Need Specific Faith
The challenge to make our prayer requests more definite needs to be tempered with Jesus' gentle reminder as this encounter draws to a close. He told Bartimaeus, "Your faith has healed you." Though Jesus took special pains to teach this blind man to ask explicitly, it wasn't a perfectly worded request that brought healing. Bartimaeus saw only because he believed he would. Answered prayer happens as God responds to our faith.

Sometimes I shake my head at how outlandish Jesus must have seemed to the religious community of His day. In an atmosphere where worship was straitlaced and duty-bound and as exciting as cold oatmeal, Jesus set off dynamite with His hilariously incredible claims. "I tell you the truth, if anyone says to this mountain, 'Go, throw yourself into the sea,' and does not doubt in his heart but believes that what he says will happen, it will be done for him" (Mark 11:23). Can't you imagine the uproar among the Pharisees when they heard that this crackpot was telling people that at their bidding God would rearrange their country's topography? But I'm sure Jesus purposely used such an extravagant illustration because He knew it would capture their attention. When everyone listened intently, He went on. "Therefore I tell you, whatever you ask for in prayer, believe that you have received it, and it will be yours" (Mark 11:24).

None of us would argue with the teaching that nothing is impossible to those who believe. The issue isn't whether or not faith matters; our struggle is with how to get more faith.

Rosalind Rinker has been greatly used of God in our generation to move people to a greater vitality in prayer. In her classic little book *Prayer, Conversing with God*, she talks about her own hunger to see her prayers answered. She tried praying God-sized requests, and saw little happen. But then she began to see that requests need to be faith-sized, not God-sized.

A faith-sized request is first of all a request which is just the right "believing" size for your faith. It is not a request which is so large that the very size of it makes you wonder if God will answer. It is a request for a particular situation, in which you pray for a special person or thing, and ask only for that which you can *really believe God will do*, in a given time limit. This does not limit what God can do, but it honestly recognizes the size of your faith. And there is every reason to believe that you will be asking for larger things as your faith grows."[1]

In the Scripture, *growing* often links up with *faith*. Have faith like a mustard seed, Jesus told His followers. Jesus didn't instruct us to have faith like a mustard *tree*. He expected us to start with the seed, and let it grow into an enormous tree. "We ought always to thank God for you, brothers, and rightly so," Paul encouraged the Thessalonians, "because your faith is growing more and more" (2 Thes. 1:3).

This pattern of progressive growth is shown first in the Old Testament. When the Children of Israel prepared to enter the Promised Land, the Lord made it clear the land would not be theirs completely in an instant. "The Lord your God will drive out those nations before you, little by little. You will not be allowed to eliminate them all at once, or the wild animals will multiply around you. But the Lord your God will deliver them over to you" (Deut. 7:22-23). A God-sized miracle was going to happen: a rag-tag rabble of former slaves would conquer a nation of giants. God's power, of course, was more than enough to accomplish this entire miracle in a moment. But instead His chosen method was "little by little." One step at a time He instructed, one battle after another, for in these battles He was transforming this band of undisciplined slaves into people who could rule the land to His glory.

If we had enough faith, God could right now pick up Mt. McKinley and throw it into the Pacific Ocean. But which of us possesses such faith? So why fill our prayer notebooks with Mt. McKinley-sized requests when we only have faith enough to see a triple-X theater closed in our town? Wiser we are to pray and *believe* for the theater's removal. And as we see God move the evil, something else moves as well—the level of our faith.

The boy David could summon faith to fell Goliath because he'd already seen God deliver him from a lion, and then a bear. Taking on the lions and the bears before us, and believing God to deliver us from them, will generate the faith to stand against Goliath when he swaggers before us. Others in the army of Israel heard the giant's boasts and longed to see him defeated, I'm sure. Quite likely many even prayed he'd be killed and assured each other that God was capable of such a feat. But perhaps these couldn't muster the faith to take on the giant themselves because they hadn't let God kill the lions in their lives. They'd not prayed for the things they could believe to see happen, so their faith had no chance to grow up to giant-killing size.

When Bartimaeus spelled out his request, he didn't ask that all the blind in Israel be healed. He didn't ask that the Romans be cast from the land. God has power to do these things, of course, but perhaps Bartimaeus knew he didn't have the faith to believe them into being. But he could believe Jesus for his sight, and his faith brought healing. Like him, we need to believe for small requests before we tackle big ones.

Jesus Will Help Us if We Persist in Prayer

When Bartimaeus heard Jesus was nearby, he began shouting. Even stern rebukes from those in the crowd couldn't shush him. As they warned him to be quiet, he only yelled louder. Maybe what he shouted wasn't phrased perfectly, but he did call for help, and kept on calling until he met the Lord.

Would that we had the tenacity of Bartimaeus! I don't know about you, but when I hear discouragement from those around me, or from the Evil One, I too quickly give up. Not Bartimaeus. He refused to quit pleading, even though no one encouraged him, and many tried to undermine his efforts. How pleased God must have been with this one who insisted Christ help him, and kept on seeking help until he received it.

When a young pastor friend of mine found himself in need of $600, he decided his best course of action would be prayer. Randy had just graduated from seminary, and had begun his first church-planting assignment. He and his wife found an apartment, but after they'd moved in, they discovered rent would be due in advance. Randy's salary from denominational headquarters wouldn't arrive until the end of the month, however, so they needed money at once from some other source. As Randy prayed, he realized this might be an opportunity for God to confirm his call to this particular ministry, so he asked the Lord to supply the $600 he needed.

The rent was due Friday afternoon, but 4 o'clock came, and no money had appeared. Unsure of what to do, Randy went to the apartment manager's office. A reprieve awaited him. The manager asked if Randy would wait until Monday to pay his rent, since they'd already made a bank deposit that day, and didn't want the check left undeposited for the weekend. Randy was more than happy to oblige, and waited eagerly to see what God was going to do.

Sunday morning, he went to church, and as he entered, he ran into an old friend leaving after the first service. When his friend asked what Randy was doing in the city, Randy began telling about the ministry he'd come to pioneer, but the second service was beginning, so the friend decided to stay so he and Randy could continue their conversation. When the offering was taken, Randy's friend wrote a check, but instead of placing it in the plate, he put it in Randy's pocket. When Randy looked at it later, the check was for $600—the exact amount he'd prayed for, even though he'd made no mention to his friend that he had any financial needs!

Like Randy, blind Bartimaeus saw God work because he believed in Christ's power, and learned to channel that power to meet his specific need. And God continues to ask His people, "What do you want Me to do for you?" May we be ready with answers that please Him.

NOTES

1. Catherine Marshall, *Adventures in Prayer* (New York: Ballantine Books, 1975), p. 12.

2. Ibid., p. 11.

3. Russ Johnston, *Dynamic Praying for Exciting Results* (Wheaton, Illinois: Tyndale House Publishers, 1979), p. 25.

4. Rosalind Rinker, *Prayer: Conversing with God* (Grand Rapids, Michigan: Zondervan Publishing House, 1959), p. 59.

CHAPTER FOUR

Jesus and the Thief

Oliver Wilcox liked to throw money around. Of course he preferred to think of it as having a penchant for quality and being willing to pay for it. Either way you looked at it, money seemed to flow from his wallet as fast as water cascades over Niagra Falls. His opulent home sported an indoor pool and his own tennis court. ("I hate to wait for a playing time at the racquet club," he explained.) His wife's closet listed more designers' names than a dozen copies of *Vogue Magazine*. His travel agent took her own Bahamas cruise, financed by the profits she picked up from booking Oliver's travels. And the amazing part of the story is this: where Oliver's money came from, no one knew. But because he seemed wealthy, credit came easily, and multiplied quickly until he owed people all over the city.

Only then did the sad truth come out. The bankroll financing Oliver's lavish lifestyle was as genuine as a child's play money. Oliver's borrowing amounted to nothing more than thievery, because he had no way to repay the money.

But the day the marshalls headed for his home to take him on fraud charges, Oliver got a phone call from the state lottery. Oliver, it seemed, had just won a record $8.5 million jackpot! His creditors got their money, and Oliver not only got off scot-free, but he ended up with a fortune. Now, that's one lucky thief, wouldn't you agree?

In reality, there is no Oliver Wilcox . . . his story was fabricated to prepare you to hear the *true* account of a robber who did come into luck even better than Oliver's. After a lifetime of rebellion against God, on his deathbed, as it were, this robber got the chance to negate all the wrong he'd done, and with nothing more than a call to Christ for help, won an eternal place for himself in Glory. You may know this man as the thief on the cross.

> Two other men, both criminals, were also led out with [Jesus] to be executed. When they came to the place called The Skull, there they crucified Him, along with the criminals—one on His right, the other on His left.
>
> One of the criminals who hung there hurled insults at Him: "Aren't You the Christ? Save Yourself and us!"
>
> But the other criminal rebuked him. "Don't you fear God," he said, "since you are under the same sentence? We are punished justly, for we are getting what our deeds deserve. But this Man has done nothing wrong."
>
> Then he said, "Jesus, remember me when you come into your kingdom."
>
> Jesus answered him, "I tell you the truth, today you will be with Me in paradise" (Luke 23:32-33, 39-43).

If this thief lived today, he'd surely get offers from

seminaries around the country to teach a class called An Introduction to Forgiveness. No one could have been more qualified! And his course outline would have certainly made clear these three principles, because they shine so clearly through his encounter with Jesus on the cross.

1. God's forgiveness is boundless.
2. Forgiveness has to be received to set us free.
3. No one can escape needing forgiveness.

God's Forgiveness Is Boundless

Which sins are bad enough to make us so depraved that God can no longer forgive us? If a pollster asked this question, what answers do you think he'd get?

There'd be those who would point to sexual sins as damnation-producers. Surely fornication, or adultery, or repeated promiscuity are sordid enough to alienate us from God's grace forever. But as soon as we'd agreed that immorality would ban us from heaven, a Bible student would remind us of Rahab, the prostitute of Jericho who hid Israel's spies. This woman was obviously a seasoned expert at the oldest profession. When the leaders of Jericho searched for the spies, they started at Rahab's house. Common sense, and common knowledge, probably told them where men traveling without their wives most often spent their evenings when they came to Jericho. But by her trust in Israel's God, Rahab came to faith, and won a place in the lineage of Jesus Christ, as Matthew 1:5 records.

If sexual sins can't overcome God's grace, how about murder? Wouldn't the cold-blooded and calculated taking of a human life stamp us as unredeemable? This answer works until we think of David, who took Uriah's wife into an adulterous affair, and then had her husband killed. Yet, after his confession, David carried the title "The Man after God's Heart."

Then what about turning away from God, and saying we want no part of Him? This is a serious sin indeed, but the disciple Peter committed it, not once, but three times; yet he found forgiveness, and went on to exemplify the rock-solid faithfulness on which Christ built His church.

This dying thief received forgiveness, even though he did nothing we might consider important to merit God's help. He didn't make restitution for what he took; he didn't sell all he had and give to the poor; he wasn't baptized; he never attended church; he didn't partake of Holy Communion. He did nothing but admit his unworthiness, believe Christ could help him, and ask for mercy. When he turned to Christ, all the sinful things he had done didn't keep him from God's life, and the total absence of any compensating acts of good didn't disqualify him from receiving grace, either.

If there is hope for this hopeless thief—and hope for Rahab, and David, and Paul, and Peter—there is hope for any of us, no matter what our sins.

Have you committed some sin you believe God can't forgive? Perhaps it's some sexual sin. Or maybe you're guilty of taking your child's life in an abortion. Maybe you've stolen, or cheated, or lied in your business or in some other relationship that matters to you. Perhaps you are guilty of a "smaller" sin, but it's one you've committed over and over and confessed hundreds of times. It's a sin God wants you to forsake, but you continue to give in, and now that you've given into it *again*, you believe there can simply be no grace left for you.

Like the thief on the cross, it took the realization of my own mortality to make me wake up to God. I lived a wild and immoral existence through my high school years. Thoughts of God were the last thing I'd have considered.

But as a Navy jet fighter pilot, I brushed up against death several times. These close encounters opened my eyes to my need for God, so one night I told Him I was willing to do His will. This commitment led to significant moral changes in my life. But even though I could see the changes, it seemed to me I'd have to even the score for all the rotten things I'd done in the past; otherwise I didn't see how God could ever forgive me. I actually went to seminary with the thought, "I've been so bad that if I'm going to make it to heaven, I'll have to be a preacher!"

But after a year in seminary, I came across a little pamphlet that helped me understand that salvation comes by faith alone. All the good we'll ever do can't earn it. This news was so wonderful I couldn't believe it! With that understanding, I gave up my struggle to earn God's favor, and accepted the forgiveness God offered freely.

Jesus said, "Whoever comes to Me I will never drive away" (John 6:37). He didn't reject the dying thief who asked to be forgiven, and He won't reject us, either. As we admit our wrongdoing, we can live each day confident that God accepts us and has forgiven us, simply because He has promised to respond to our faith and desire to follow Him.

Forgiveness Must Be Received to Set Us Free

Two thieves, not just one, died on crosses beside Jesus. Both faced eternity, and both were within reach of God's own Son. One turned to Christ and received the promise of heaven; the other died in rebellion to face condemnation. One submitted to the Lord; the other mocked Him.

Both John and Gary served in the war in Vietnam. For John, life in the twenty years since has been intermittent hell. For years, he slept with a loaded gun under his pillow. Terrifying nightmares still steal his sleep. His wife has endured undeserved anger and sullenness and depression and even physical abuse. He takes wild and reckless chances with his physical safety. "Why not?" he says, laughing, to his wife when she cautions him. "Life can be snuffed out in a minute anyway. Why try to protect it?" John's wife believes the war ruined their lives, and they'll find no escape for the rest of their lives from the emotional wounds it inflicted.

Gary Bucher's Vietnam years set the stage for an opposite direction for his life. Like John, he went to Vietnam a rash and rebellious kid. And as a Marine machine gunner, he was part of the same confusion, and terror, and killing that John experienced there. But in the twenty years since, he hides no gun under his pillow, and nightmares don't plague him. He's become a minister of the Gospel, and travels around the United States with his wife, telling others how getting shot in Vietnam paved the way for his beginning a new life in God.

During an experience which ruined one man, the other was saved, because he accepted the help God had to offer. Circumstances can either make or break us, depending on what we decide to do with the resource God holds out to us. Only one thief gained eternity, because only one chose to accept Christ's deliverance.

A choice to receive God's help can open our spiritual eyes to truths we couldn't see before.

Myrl Glockner suffered a number of miscarriages and stillborn babies before it became clear she and her husband Bob would never have children of their own. Myrl remembered one of the early losses, the death of a tiny premature son they named Robby, as a turning point in deciding how she would deal with the losses.

"When the doctor first told me I might lose the baby, everything in me wanted to shout, 'No! I *want* this baby, and I will have this baby—whether God decides to help me or not!'

"But in the three days that followed, as I lay immobile [in the hospital] waiting for an outcome I knew I couldn't control, I had time to think and to remember Jesus in the Garden of Gethsemane, facing an agonizing death on the cross. He could ask His Father to spare Him the pain, but He said instead, 'Not *My* will, but Yours be done.'

"I needed to release my child to God with a commitment that whatever the outcome of his life, I would trust God to do right and that good would come to us all through it. Once I said yes to God, that He could do with my child's life what He thought best, incredible peace flooded through me.

"And over time, I began to see Him take the hurt and use it as a vehicle to develop a new sensitivity and a new tenderness in me, both toward God and toward others who were hurting. Instead of hardening me, the sorrow made me softer and better equipped for the life I was being called to lead."[1]

Now, a number of years after her children's deaths, Myrl still feels a sense of loss as she remembers, but the pain is gone, and in its place is honest joy.

"It's not that I'm glad for the suffering itself," she says. "But God has taken that suffering and through it produced so much good that I am glad for having gone through those losses. This deeper pain has somehow opened in me a capacity for deeper joy."

What about the hurt you now face? These pains may be the very instrument that bring you into the peace and joy for which you hunger. When we meet this thief in heaven, I fully expect he'll report, "The best thing that happened to me was my crucifixion, for without it, I might not have trusted my life to Christ! Without it, I might have suffered a little less on earth, but I would have missed heaven!" Your illness, or broken relationship, or disappointment, or lost job, or loved one's death can be the cross that brings you more deeply into the life of Christ, if you choose to let God meet you in your pain.

No One Can Escape Needing Forgiveness

People respond to this story of Jesus and the dying thief with enthusiasm or skepticism—they either love it or they can't appreciate it. There is no middle ground. Christ's grace plays like sweet music to the ears of some. They would appreciate the gunfighter who made his "death-bed" repentance when he was shot off his horse. As the story goes, his tombstone read, "Between the saddle and the ground, he mercy sought and mercy found." To me, that's cutting it a little close!

But to another crowd, this yarn becomes a mockery rather than music. These are the good folk who didn't wait for their deathbeds to reach out for salvation. Perhaps they've spent most of a lifetime in faithful service to the Lord. At times that service has seemed to demand their dearest and their best. These believers didn't "drink or smoke or chew, or run around with them that do"! To these sacrificing saints, it seems grossly unfair that a ne'er-do-well who has languished in sin all his life can repent at the last second, and receive a heavenly entrance, just as they have.

Among this group of grumblers, you'd see some familiar faces. The Prodigal Son's elder brother would surely be there. Remember him? When his father threw a welcoming party to celebrate the Prodigal's return, this eldest son refused to come. "Look! All these years I've been slaving for you and never disobeyed your orders. Yet you never gave me even a young goat so I could celebrate with my friends. But when this no-good-brother of mine who has squandered your property with prostitutes comes home, you kill the fattened calf for him!" (Luke 15:29-30) It seemed so unfair.

Another group who'd arrive with picket signs held high and crying "Unfair!" would be the workers of Matthew 20 who agreed to pick grapes all day in return for one denarius in payment. All was fine, until they lined up to receive their wages at the day's end, and discovered those who didn't start work until just before quitting time received the same wage they did. And they exploded! "These men who were hired last worked only one hour," they said, "and you have made them equal to us who have borne the burden of the work and the heat of the day." I'd be grumbling too, wouldn't you? Where is the justice in such a decision?

The Apostle Peter would likely be there also. Jesus told Peter what his final days would be like, and how did Peter respond? He turned toward John, and asked, "Lord, what about him? Is he going to have it easier, or harder? Will I be more blessed or less blessed than he? Will he suffer more, or less? I won't know if the future You have for me is fair or not until I compare it to the struggles and rewards John is going to get."

Do you sympathize with the Prodigal's brother, and with the hardworking grape-pickers, and with Peter? Sometimes I do. But when I grumble about what seems to be God's lack of fair play, I feel the Holy Spirit's nudge, reminding me of an evil he hates as much as any other, the evil of comparison.

The elder brother was happy with his father's generosity until he compared his lot to what his brother received. One denarius for a day's work sounded like fair pay until the all-day workers compared their wage to those who only worked a short time. And Peter refused to gladly accept the Lord's direction for him until he could compare it with another disciple's lot.

This evil of comparison leads to jealousy, envy, and ungratefulness. That's why Paul tells us that "we do not

dare to classify or compare ourselves with some who com-
mend themselves. When they measure themselves by
themselves and compare themselves with themselves, they
are not wise" (2 Cor. 10:12).

When we compare ourselves to each other, we're strug-
gling to climb a ladder that's leaning against the wrong
wall, because God's standard of righteousness isn't any
person—it's Jesus Christ Himself. Looking at each other
to determine our goodness is a little like two fleas fighting
over which of them is closer to the moon. One may be
standing on top of Mt. McKinley, while the other may sit
at the bottom of the Grand Canyon, but when they compare their relative standing to the distance involved in
lunar travel, both fall so ridiculously short that the mountain and the valley become irrelevant.

And that's how it is with us. Maybe I've served God for
twenty years; you for only one. But compared to the per-
fection of Jesus Christ, the best either of us can offer falls
so laughably short of the mark we may as well discount it
completely. Instead of being amazed God let the dying
thief into heaven, those of us who have followed Him for
decades should be so amazed He lets *us* in we've no time
to even consider anyone else's credentials!

When we've seen the majesty and holiness of God for
ourselves, there's no more talk about who is better than
whom. We fall on our faces—as did Isaiah when he saw
the Lord—and cry, "Woe to me! . . . I am ruined! For I
am a man of unclean lips, and I live among a people of
unclean lips, and my eyes have seen the King, the Lord
Almighty" (Isa. 6:5). When we've seen God, we're no
longer aware of others' sinfulness; we're painfully aware
only of our own, aware enough to cry, "Woe is *me.*"

If the dying thief couldn't qualify for God's forgiveness, we'd all be done for, because by God's evaluation,
we're all dying thieves. There is no hierarchy to heaven;

all that's required to relate to God is acceptance of His gift of life by faith. And all that's required for a life of blessing is continuing to accept His gifts by faith. Of course, faith that is real results in actions. If the dying thief had been miraculously spared, I believe he would have come off that cross to live a different life. When the eternal genuinely invades the mortal, changes happen. They must. But the changes only confirm our faith; they don't create it. Paul explains this in Titus 3:4-5: "When the kindness and love of God our Saviour appeared, He saved us, not because of righteous things we had done, but because of His mercy."

When Peter tried to compare his standing to John's, Jesus said this to him: "If I want him to remain alive until I return, what is that to you? *You must follow Me*" (John 21:22, italics added). We need to compare ourselves to God's expectations for us . . . and nothing, or no one else. And when it appears God is generous to a less-deserving one, we need to rejoice in His generosity, knowing full well we deserve nothing from His hand.

These are the lessons of Forgiveness 101, taught to us by a man who had nothing to offer God but his need and his faith. This course may appear to be a simple one, but it's certainly not optional. Passing it is required to graduate from our pain on earth, to peace, and a solid hope of heaven to come.

NOTES

1. Maureen J. Rank, *Free to Grieve* (Minneapolis: Bethany House Publishers, 1985), pp. 166-167.

CHAPTER FIVE

Jesus and the Lady Who Wouldn't Take No for an Answer

Nancy Shelley is thirty-four years old, married, the mother of two small children, and a victim of multiple sclerosis. Her doctors warn her to expect gradual deterioration which will eventually leave her an invalid. Her Christian friends pray for healing, but the disease appears only to be getting worse. What should Nancy Shelley believe about prayer?

Neil Wilson's wife filed for divorce two years ago. With his divorce papers, Neil was also served notice he'd no longer be welcome as a speaker on the Christian conference circuit. In two years, he's lost his wife, his children, his home, his source of income, and his ministry. Though he's tried hard to "get over" Natalie and get on with his life, his biggest desire is that they be reunited. He's prayed, fasted, confessed his sins, tried to change, thanked God for the trial, gone through the laying on of hands for healing; in short, done everything he can think of to move heaven on his behalf, yet God remains silent. What do we tell Neil about getting answers from God?

Dale McGregor weighs sixty-five pounds more than he

should, but he simply cannot stop eating. His food addiction is undermining his self-confidence, limiting his effectiveness on the job, and generating endless fights with his wife. Dale has dieted, of course, but he loses only to find the pounds again. He's prayed prayers of helplessness, and prayers of affirmation, and prayers of release. None seem to elicit any response from God at all.

Two thousand years ago, there was a woman from Syrophonesia who would have understood Nancy, and Neil, and Dale very well. A demon was destroying this woman's child. But instead of letting desperation drive her to despair, she confronted Jesus with her need. Her faith overcame massive obstacles and coaxed a silent and seemingly reluctant Christ into healing her child. The secrets she knew about prayer may change the way you bring your requests to God, and open the way for answers in the desperations of your life.

Jesus withdrew to the region of Tyre and Sidon. A Canaanite woman from that vicinity came to Him, crying out, "Lord, Son of David, have mercy on me! My daughter is suffering terribly from demon-possession."

Jesus did not answer a word. So His disciples came to Him and urged Him, "Send her away, for she keeps crying out after us."

He answered, "I was sent only to the lost sheep of Israel."

The woman came and knelt before Him. "Lord, help me!" she said.

He replied, "It is not right to take the children's bread and toss it to their dogs."

"Yes, Lord," she said, "but even the dogs eat the crumbs that fall from their masters' table."

Then Jesus answered, "Woman, you have great

faith! Your request is granted." And her daughter was healed from that very hour (Matt. 15:21-39).

This Canaanite woman refused to take no for an answer, and wound up with her request granted and Christ praising her faith. What can we learn from her example? I believe there are four lessons that we can draw from her story.

She Let Desperation Drive Her to Determination
Are you experiencing desperation in any area of life? Is your child hurting from illness, or rebellion, or a destructive lifestyle? Maybe you feel desperate for your marriage or your business. Or perhaps you struggle alone against some personal demon you can't conquer, such as lust, or jealousy, or drinking, or covetousness, or anger. If what you're feeling can't be described by anything less than desperation, you stand in very good company. Desperation seems to be the fertile soil in which persistence can take root.

It's laudable to pray for the leaders of our nation, and the homeless in our cities, and we should. But if you want to learn to persist in prayer, *start* with needs about which you feel personally desperate, as did this Canaanite woman.

In Christ's major teaching on persistence in prayer in Luke 11, the person Christ chose to praise (and encourage us to emulate!) was a man with his back to the wall and no way out. This man had unexpected guests and no food in the house. And remember, this was before 7-11s, and 24-hour Big Boys existed. So if this host couldn't borrow provisions from a friend, the guests would have to go hungry, and he would be humiliated. The man was desperate enough to risk imposing on and angering his friend to get the bread he needed. His desperation pushed him to persist until he left with his arms filled with groceries, and Jesus praised him for it.

In Genesis 32, Jacob wrestled with God all night, refusing to give up until God blessed him. Jacob's bulldog stance resulted in God unloading blessing upon him, and a new name for Jacob, the Deceiver. God called him Israel, *he who wrestles with God, and prevails*. But what drove Jacob to act so boldly with God? The text indicates it may have been more desperation than anything else. This wrestling match with the Divine took place the night before Jacob was to meet his brother Esau, from whom he'd stolen the birthright years before. Jacob fully expected Esau to kill him and his entire household. From this mental framework of desperation, Jacob found the wherewithal to wrestle with God, and to prevail. We can be people of great faith, or simply incredibly desperate. It appears either will produce actions that move God to work on our behalf. Your panic may be more an asset than a liability!

After Randy Pope, a young friend of mine, graduated from seminary, he moved to Atlanta determined to start a church. Over the next six months, he gathered a congregation, and they began to pray for a place to meet regularly. And together they set a date by which they were expecting God to answer.

The date came . . . and went . . . but the group had no prospects at all for a meeting place. Randy felt desperate. Maybe his little group would grow disheartened and question the reality of a God who provides for the needs of His children. But instead of letting his panic drive him to despair, Randy turned it to more intense seeking for God and His plan.

Then an idea came. Randy had heard that the owner of an Atlanta-based hotel chain was a Christian. Perhaps he'd be able to help. Fearful that his request for an appointment with the man would be rejected, Randy went straight to his office. As he entered the office, the man's secretary wasn't at her desk, and the executive's door was ajar. That was enough leading for Randy! He introduced himself to the hotel owner, and presented his need. The man showed sympathy, and offered use of a meeting space in one of his corporate office buildings for only $50 a month! Randy later discovered the facility usually rented for *$2,000 a month*. God's abundant provision ignited the church's faith, and from that simple beginning, it has grown to five congregations. Instead of despairing when the expected answer didn't come, Randy let his panic fuel determination, and saw God do a mighty work.

The Canaanite woman also had a choice. She could have let her desperation disintegrate to despair, or she could use it to drive her on to persistent, insistent, powerful prayer. She chose the latter, and against enormous odds, won her case with God.

She Didn't Assume God's Silence Meant No

Have you ever cried to the Lord for help, only to feel that your prayers are trying to get through clouds of solid cement? If you have, you find yourself in good company. This desperate mother came to Jesus, pleading for help for her daughter, but Jesus did not answer a word.

And look at Job. Through 36 chapters of Job's suffering, God is as silent as a tax evader at an IRS audit. He offers no explanation, no comfort, no deliverance, nothing.

The Apostle Paul had the same experience. In his second letter to the church at Corinth, he tells of how he sought God for deliverance from a pain he described as a thorn in his flesh. We're not sure what this thorn was. Some scholars believe it to be his failing eyesight; others have suggested physical maladies like migraines, malaria, or epilepsy. But whatever it was, we do know he came to God three different times to take it away. God refused Paul an instant and easy answer.

But here's the point that gives us courage. For each of these seekers, we've been allowed to hear the end of the story. And for each, the story concluded with God not only hearing, but answering their prayers to their satisfaction. With the Canaanite woman, her answer came just as she requested it; Jesus healed her daughter. God not only delivered Job from his illness, but restored his fortune and family. God increased all that he had double, and, the Scripture records, "The Lord blessed the latter part of Job's life more than the first" (Job 42:12).

Paul was never healed of his thorn, but the answer God did give more than satisfied him. Paul reported, "He said to me, 'My grace is sufficient for you, for My power is made perfect in weakness'" (2 Cor. 12:9). This word from God so met Paul's need that he actually began to brag about his weakness. He became proud of it, because it became the place in which God's power became most evident in his life.

When God is silent, we too quickly assume His answer is no. We give up before God has the chance to do all He wants in us and through us, as He works to answer our prayers. Don't assume a negative answer, just because God is saying nothing. The Canaanite woman kept on crying out, and because she did, she won her case with God.

But be careful of other believers encouraging you to give up. Instead of shoring up this Canaanite woman's faith, Christ's disciples urged Him to send her away.

Other Christians may discourage you because they don't have faith themselves. Or maybe, like Job's wife, it's too hard on them to see you struggle. But maybe they'll discourage you because God's reluctance is causing them terrible public relations problems. It can be very embarrassing to Christian workers when the Lord doesn't seem to come through for His children.

Take it from one who knows. I remember early in my ministry, when a troubled businessman visited our church. On the way out of the service, he grabbed my hand, and said, "I need to see you." We met that afternoon and he spent an hour telling me about his problems. I spent fifteen minutes telling him about Christ, and he gave his life to the Lord. Then we went and talked to his family, and they trusted Christ too! Was I excited! I finished the day by giving him clear assurance that now everything was fine since he was right with God, and he could expect all of his business troubles to clear up.

Well, they didn't. We prayed, and I encouraged him, and we prayed some more, but his business spiraled downward. About this time, one of my seminary professors was coming to town, so I saw a way out. "We'll talk to Dr. George," I told the businessman. "He'll show us why we aren't getting God's solution to this problem."

So off to Dr. George we trudged, and poured out my friend's tale of woe. As we finished, I looked at Dr. George for the profound theological key to open heaven's door and get an answer for my friend. "Well," the seminarian replied thoughtfully, "it just takes some apples longer to bake than others."

As you can guess, this young Christian beside me was not terribly helped by this profound perspective, even though it held a germ of truth. And I was embarrassed for God's sake. I'd promised my friend a God of instant rescue; what he received was a cooking lesson.

God's silence and apparent reluctance can embarrass His children, so don't always count on them for encouragement as you persist in prayer.

When Christ Did Speak, the Woman Listened

When Christ did acknowledge the woman, His words must have fallen like lead on her heart. "I was sent only to the lost sheep of Israel," He said; then He added, "It is not right to take the children's bread and toss it to their dogs."

How would you like an answer like this from the great prophet to whom you had bared your soul? He made it clear she belonged to the wrong group to receive help from Him, and to add insult to injury, He compared her to a dog. I think I would have been furious. A dog, indeed! And I likely would have stomped away. Or else I'd have slunk away to find the nearest pity party so I could wimper about my unworthiness and Jesus' lack of compassion. Either way, I'd have missed the answer I sought.

Not this woman. Jesus didn't say what she wanted to hear, but she listened anyway, and agreed with Him. "Yes, Lord, You're right. I am unworthy of Your help. I don't deserve to have You grant my request."

However, it doesn't appear that this quiet humility characterized her from the beginning of the encounter. She came to Jesus loudly demanding He drop everything and heal her daughter. When He didn't respond, she created enough of a fuss that the disciples were embarrassed. Only in the face of Jesus' reluctance did she come and kneel before Him in a stance much more appropriate to a subject coming to petition her king.

Christ held back the answer to her prayer, and consequently this woman changed from a God-user to a God-worshiper. If Christ had jumped to obey at this insistent mother's first demand, she would have missed a life-changing experience of coming to a deeper personal submission to the Master of her own life. Because of how Christ dealt with her, he became her own Lord, not just her daughter's healer.

In your desperate request, have you ever acknowledged that God doesn't owe you a thing? Have you ever said, "Lord, there is no reason why You should help me. I am a sinner. But I understand You love me anyway, and You sent Your Son to die for this dog. I come, not pleading any merit of my own, but simply pleading that Your Son died for sinners like me."

David stands as our example of this kind of humility. Though he prayed some of the most aggressive, confident, even pushy prayers recorded in Scripture, he was quick to remind himself, "When my heart was grieved and my spirit embittered, I was senseless and ignorant; I was a brute beast before You. Yet I am always with You; You hold me by my right hand. You guide me with Your counsel, and afterward You will take me into glory" (Ps. 73:21-24).

David, and our Canaanite friend, didn't dispute with God. They didn't whine, or accuse Him of playing favorites, or slander His character. They admitted their unworthiness, but they used that very unworthiness to remind Him of His grace.

She Demonstrated Unrelenting Faith
Once this desperate woman had agreed with God about her position before Him, she didn't turn and give up, as we might have done. Submission to God's power and sovereignty doesn't leave us weak and passive. It gives us a solid standing on which to argue and poke and persist and believe right on through to the answer for which we have sought.

Jesus had told the Canaanite woman it was God's will that He give Himself only to Israel. Was He right? Of course He was! Although His eventual mission would include the salvation of the whole world, He had been instructed by His Father to spend His earthly years wooing

Israel. It was through those in Israel who responded to Him that God intended to take His light to the world. From Old Testament times Israel had been called to be a light to the nations. Consistent with His purposes, God first called those of Israel to Himself.

Thus the earthly mission of Jesus was limited to Israel. It would not have been the will of God that He heal this woman's daughter at the expense of His initial call to those in Israel. And the woman agreed with His right to make that decision. He was, after all, the Master, and she was the seeker. She did not dispute with Him, but she also did not assume a "no" when none was clearly spoken. Christ explained why He must be reluctant in helping her, but nowhere did He say He wouldn't. That lack of a clear "no" was just the crack in the door this woman needed. " 'Yes, Lord,' she said, '*but* even the dogs eat the crumbs that fall from their masters' table' " (Matt. 15:27, italics added).

She turned and used the Lord's own illustration to argue her case. "Of course a good master would never feed the dogs the food that rightfully belongs to his children! I certainly don't want You to do that, Lord! Give to Israel all that they will receive of Your goodness. But I'm not asking for their blessing, Lord. All I want is just a crumb. A good master won't feed the dogs the children's food, but surely he won't scrape up what the children don't eat and throw it away. In his kindness, he'll feed his dogs too, won't he?"

How could Christ resist such a compelling argument? Now instead of fighting against Him, she wrestled *with* Him, in accordance with His purposes, and she prevailed. Persistence in prayer doesn't mean simply droning your request over and over until God sickens of hearing it. Instead, it means providing Him with ample reason to circumvent the boundaries He has set for Himself. The

Canaanite woman provided the justification Jesus needed to say yes to her, even though God's intent at this point in history was that Christ focus His energies on Israel. She allowed Him to do what He wanted, to expand His earthly mission to include her. In doing so, she won His high praise.

"Woman," Jesus told her, "you have great faith! Your request is granted." To which of the disciples did Jesus ever pay such a compliment?

P.T. Forsyth, in his book *The Soul of Prayer* (Eerdmans), makes this startling statement:

> Prayer is wrestling with God. . . . We say too soon, 'Thy will be done'; and too ready acceptance of a situation as His will often means feebleness or sloth. It may be His will that we surmount His will. Resisting His will may be doing His will. . . ."

If this mother had given up at Christ's silence, or had gone home after His explanation that He'd been sent only to Israel, she'd have missed God's best for her. And Christ would have missed the opportunity to show the wonder of His grace which extends even to those most unworthy of His help. Because of her persistence, the woman learned deeper submission to a Master, and He was given opportunity to give His disciples a glimpse into grace that would extend even beyond Israel to anyone who would come to Him in faith.

How we need to learn to persist in prayer! We need to keep on praying, even in the face of God's silence. If His answer falls cold on our hearts, we need to hear and change in the way He asks us to. But if He still has not said no, we need to keep on asking, keep on arguing, keep on persisting. This is the wrestling prayer that gets results and brings glory to God.

CHAPTER SIX

Jesus and the Determined Doubter

Some surnames have been so often associated with a particular characteristic that the two have become inseparable. To illustrate, try your hand at my version of The Name Game, by filling in the name you know goes in each blank.

- Little Orphan _____
- _____ the Kid
- Calamity _____
- Too Tall _____
- Diamond _____
- Buffalo _____
- _____ the Ripper
- Doubting _____

Sadly enough, you may have found the answer easiest to get was the last one: Doubting Thomas. Poor Thomas! For 2,000 years his name lives on, but is he known for heroic conquests or laudable faith? No, his claim to fame springs from his finely honed skills as a skeptic.

63

We're quick to hold Thomas up as an example of what not to do, but I suspect many of us identify much more with Thomas and his doubts than we care to admit. Maybe we're so hard on Thomas because he pushes us up against a part of ourselves we'd just as soon ignore. After all, what room can there be to entertain doubt in the household of faith?

If you are a Thomas-in-hiding, the close encounter you are about to confront may give you the courage to leave your closet for good. Jesus dealt kindly and patiently with this doubter and brought him to a faith so staunch it propelled Thomas to transform India with the Gospel.

Now Thomas (called Didymus), one of the Twelve, was not with the disciples when Jesus came. When the other disciples told him that they had seen the Lord, he declared, "Unless I see the nail marks in His hands and put my finger where the nails were, and put my hand into His side, I will not believe it."

A week later His disciples were in the house again, and Thomas was with them. Though the doors were locked, Jesus came and stood among them and said, "Peace be with you!" Then He said to Thomas, "Put your finger here; see My hands. Reach out your hand and put it into My side. Stop doubting and believe."

Thomas said to Him, "My Lord and my God!"

Then Jesus told him, "Because you have seen Me, you have believed; blessed are those who have not seen and yet have believed" (John 20:24-29).

We Need More Believing Doubters
Among Christian circles, doubt is about as desirable as a good case of head lice. We're as likely to wish for doubters in our midst as we are to hope for an IRS audit.

Maybe doubt has gotten such bad press because we assume it's synonymous with disbelief and discouragement and disillusionment. Doubt deadens faith, and we want no part of it!

But did you know that the Greek word for doubt can also mean "to discriminate"? If there's anything we need in these confusing and troubled times, it's Christians with the good sense to discriminate, to listen and consider and ask questions before they jump on this new teaching or that, or before they take off after this new preacher or that. This kind of holy discrimination is what John called for when he challenged, "Dear friends, *do not believe* every spirit, but test the spirits to see whether they are from God, because many false prophets have gone out into the world" (1 John 4:1).

Did you know that "do *not* believe" was ever commanded in Scripture? Being a believer doesn't mean we're to naively and gullibly embrace every idea that sounds the least bit God-oriented. Scripture warns us that Satan specializes in deceit, even disguising himself as an angel of light. In this generation, when cults and occult influences abound, when movie stars take up prime television time to convince us their encounters with extraterrestrials have led to "dancing in the light," we should all look at ways to acquire a dose of the doubt that discerns.

Paul praised the Berean Church for having the good sense to exercise discriminating doubt. They received the word with "readiness of mind," Paul reported. They were open and eager to hear and obey God's Word to them. But when they heard Paul's message, instead of running to the back of the auditorium to sign up for his tape series, they went home and "examined the Scriptures every day to see if what Paul said was true" (Acts 17:11). They checked what he taught against the Scriptures before they swore allegiance to it.

Mike is a Berean brand of doubter. Fifteen years ago, when the craze for jogging first swept the country, Mike didn't hotfoot it to the nearest sports store for a pair of leather Adidas. He sorted through the enthusiast's propaganda until he hit upon Dr. Cooper and his good-sense approach to Air Force fitness through aerobics. Then he observed the joggers who were trying it, to see what worked and what didn't. And he thought through his lifestyle and exercise needs. The decision to start jogging didn't happen in a high-adrenaline rush of emotion. It came slowly, but it did come.

Now, a decade and a half later, most of Mike's jogging friends have fallen by the quarter-mile-trackside. Not Mike. Three or four times a week, he still pulls on his running shoes and takes to the street, just as he has through nearly all of the last fifteen years and most likely will for the next fifteen. He didn't choose quickly because when he did, he knew he was making a commitment he'd keep for life.

Mike approaches his spiritual life the same way. Recently the men's Bible study he belongs to listened to a new series on prayer by a Dallas preacher. Though the men raved about the teachings, Mike's responses were more often quiet questions. Later, he and some of the other men took three days off work to visit the man's church in Dallas, and find out more. In the process of dealing with his doubts of discernment, Mike became convinced the prayer challenges were true, so he's changing how he prays.

But Mike decided slowly, because he intended the decision to last. He's like the wise man Jesus described in Luke 14 who doesn't build a tower without counting the cost. In this, I believe he is like his Berean brothers and sisters. They searched the Scriptures to be sure of Paul's teaching, because they were prepared to adjust their whole mode of living to conform to the teachings, if the words proved to be of God.

Notice, of course, that these Bereans went at their doubting energized by hearts hungry to hear and do God's bidding. The Pharisees of Jesus' day were doubters too, but their doubts prompted Jesus to call them "white-washed tombs" and "sons of devils," because they tolerated no hunger to be God's people. They cared nothing for obedience to God, so their doubts led them, and others, away from truth, not toward it. And it is their brand of biting, sarcastic, faith-destroying cynicism Jesus condemned when He spoke so firmly against doubt.

This brand of debilitating doubt we can do without, but may the discriminating doubters like Mike and the Bereans increase! They can be the deeper seekers in our midst who will keep us moving toward God's truth. Jesus made room for Thomas within the circle of His chosen twelve, and didn't reject him, even when he doubted the Resurrection.

Of course, doubts can also be a convenient place to hide, so we don't have to commit ourselves to truth. A posture of skepticism can be a holy-sounding way to keep ourselves on the fence, and out of the arena of faith. Jesus knew this, and He worked to purify Thomas' tendency to destructive doubting, but He never rejected Thomas just because he doubted. The Pharisees never seemed to have any doubts about their beliefs, but as someone has observed, "Those who think they have all the answers probably don't know how many questions there are!"

Lest we become too enthralled with the virtues of doubt, we do need to remember that most of the time, our doubts aren't noble attempts at discernment. They are clear and obstinate refusals to accept what God has said is true.

Unbelief can inhibit Christ from working as He wants to, and can wreak havoc with our spiritual lives. In the case of Thomas, doubt kept him from entering into the joy of the Resurrection victory, and it brought him a rebuke from the Lord.

Godly questioning helps us to listen until we're sure we've heard the Lord's voice. Unbelief hears God speak, but keeps protesting "yes, but" and "what about" and "what if" in an attempt to keep from having to *act* on God's instructions. May we encourage the art of godly questioning, but when God speaks, we need to put aside our questions and move out into His will, by faith. Christ rose from the dead, but Thomas chose not to believe Him. Doubts like his need to be put to death, lest they extinguish the fire of our faith.

To Dispel Doubt, Know Its Source
What causes unbelief? Scripture points out a number of culprits.

Being alone can cause us to doubt God. After His resurrection, Jesus appeared to His disciples. But Thomas wasn't there. Whether he was off sulking in self-pity after the disappointment of Christ's death, we don't know. But whatever the reason, the other ten disciples hung together, but Thomas didn't. You can't be a soldier of faith and the Lone Ranger at the same time. The community of Christ's people can nourish faith; isolation can destroy it.

Thomas' example also warns us that some of us have *negative personalities* that tend more easily to doubt. Before this climactic episode with Jesus, Thomas is sketched two other times in the Gospels. Back when Jesus got word His friend Lazarus was ill, He waited several days before He went to Bethany to help. Perhaps to the disciples, this decision was a wise one, since Bethany was just outside of

Jerusalem, and the Jewish leaders had threatened Jesus with death at their last encounter. But when Jesus finally announced that they would go to Bethany, Thomas spoke up. "Let us also go, that we may die with Him" (John 11:16).

Thomas looked at the situation and saw only the dark side. There could be no possibility of divine protection, or a change of heart for the Pharisees, or any other option but the worst possible scenario: they would all most certainly die. You've known people like Thomas, the parent whose child gets straight A's and who worries it will make her a perfectionist; people who see that church attendance is up and groan that they'll soon have to finance a new building program; people who inherit $20,000 and insist the taxes on it will break them. Tell them every cloud has a silver lining, and they'll remind you of how much silver has plummeted in price the last few years. Thomas probably would have.

At the Last Supper, Jesus encouraged His disciples with these words. "Where I go you know, and the way you know." Thomas was quick to correct him. "Lord, we don't know where You are going, so how can we know the way?" (John 14:5) No ambiguities for Thomas. Save the mysteries. Omit the generalities. Instruction had to be spelled out in black and white, listed in chronological order, and delivered with three carbons. To satisfy Thomas, God and His ways had to be carefully boxed, and once settled, the box locked tight for all eternity.

Later, Thomas refused to believe the other disciples' report of Christ's resurrection. It made no difference Thomas had just spent three years with these men, knowing them inside and out. Nor did it phase his dogged unbelief that the opinions on the Resurrection stood ten to one against him. Thomas the Unbending would accept only one proof of Christ's resurrection; he had to touch the Lord's wounds himself. God would have to bend to Thomas' criteria for faith because Thomas had no intention of bending to the proofs God had offered in the testimony of his ten most trusted friends. "Not good enough," Thomas said, in effect, to God. "You'll have to do better than that if I'm to believe."

To a personality with this much negativism and rigidity, doubts come easily and can barely be pried loose with a two-ton crowbar.

Taking our eyes off Jesus can transform the most faithful among us into doubters. When Peter saw Jesus walking toward him on the water, the disciple hopped out of the boat to walk to meet his Master. But then Peter chanced to look around, instead of at Christ, and the size of the waves swelling and crashing around him drowned out his faith, and he began to sink.

Stressful circumstances can generate doubt. No one had been quicker than John the Baptist to affirm Jesus' claim to deity. But after King Herod threw this godly man in prison, doubts overcame John, and he sent messengers to ask Jesus whether or not He was actually the Messiah. Solitary confinement in a dank prison and the threat of death produced enough pressure to eat away at John's faith.

Doubt can grow from *fear and a sense of inadequacy*. When God called Gideon to lead Israel in an uprising against the Midianites who had devastated them, He found Gideon hiding inside a winepress, trying to thresh some handfuls of wheat before the Midianites stole it from him. When an angel announced to Gideon that the Lord was with him, Gideon replied, "Oh, yeah?" (Or, to quote more precisely, "If the Lord is with us, why has all this happened to us?") The Lord called him a valiant warrior, to which Gideon argued, "How can I save Israel? My clan is the weakest in Manasseh, and I am the least in my family" (Jud. 6:13, 15). Gideon did at last overcome his doubts, but only after God performed three clear miracles at his request, and then sent a special outpouring of His Spirit to turn this reluctant leader into a conqueror. Why we didn't dub him "Doubting Gideon," I'm not sure. Gideon certainly outdid Thomas in showing reluctance to believe. Perhaps that only illustrates what powerful opponents to faith fear and a sense of inadequacy can be.

Fatigue is a guaranteed belief-destroyer. In a massive demonstration of faith few of us will match in a lifetime, Elijah showed God's power to defeat 450 prophets of Baal. But just after this massive victory recorded in 1 Kings 18 and 19, he got word from Queen Jezebel she'd determined to kill him. At this word Elijah became so doubt-filled, he slunk off into the wilderness, collapsed under a juniper tree, and begged to die. What happened to our giant of faith? Chances are good that part of his change of heart came from sheer fatigue. After the exhausting encounter with Baal's prophets, he ran 17 miles from Mount Carmel back to the city. Likely the combination of emotional and physical exhaustion made him a prime candidate for his faith to be crowded out by doubts. He complained he was the only one serving God in Israel; God responded there were 7,000 who had never bowed to Baal. Haven't you had times when weariness has made your problems look 7,000 times worse than what they were? I have.

God's solution for His weary servant? An angel came and instructed him to take a nap—and then another one! One theologian has said, "If I felt I were losing my faith, I would lie down until I got over it." That's often good advice.

Other people can cause us to doubt. God had set the Promised Land before His people, and told them to go in and take what He had already secured for them, but they doubted, and failed. Why? "Our brothers have made us lose heart. They say, 'The people are stronger and taller than we are; the cities are large, with walls up to the sky' " (Deut. 1:28).

It wasn't their enemies that discouraged God's people; it was their own brothers. And we're often guilty of the same sin. "Isn't that idea a little impractical?" we warn each other. Or, "We tried that two years ago, and it didn't work." We caution each other out of our faith.

James 1 makes it clear that *double-mindedness* can cause doubt to germinate. It describes the one who doubts as being "like the surf of the sea driven and tossed by the wind" and "unstable in all he does," and it promises this doubter can be sure he won't receive anything from the Lord. What stirs the doubts? In James 1:8 we read it is being a "double-minded man."

Double-mindedness means not making a commitment to follow the Lord. I want His help, but only if He doesn't ask too much. I want His guidance, but only if His directions don't call me to anything that makes me uncomfortable. Double-mindedness is like launching a boat without being willing to go aboard and sail it. Such a lack of commitment, James says, is guaranteed to produce a failing faith, just as surely as a boat without a sailor is bound to run aground.

Doubting can originate from a number of sources, and obliterating doubt isn't easy. Sometimes it seems that nothing less than an act of God can help those of us who doubt as fiercely as Thomas did. But Christ helped Thomas to find faith, and He can—and will—help us as we struggle against unbelief.

God Will Help Our Doubts if We Seek Him
Thomas insisted on the Lord's appearance, and Jesus complied. He even invited Thomas to fulfill his every

requirement, even to putting his hands into Christ's wounds. This revelation was enough for even Thomas, and he fell in worship at Jesus' feet, declaring, "My Lord, and my God!"

We see Thomas' faith as an obvious and irresistible response to Christ's appearance, but it wasn't. Had Thomas not had any heart toward God, even the bodily proof of the resurrected Christ would not have been enough to convince him. Jesus told the story of the beggar Lazarus who died and went to Abraham's bosom; and his wealthy counterpart who ended up in Hades. The rich man begged God to send Lazarus to warn his five brothers, lest they too wind up in torment. "If someone goes to them from the dead, they will repent!" the rich man asserted. But in Jesus' story, Abraham disagreed. "If they do not listen to Moses and the Prophets, they will not be convinced even if someone rises from the dead" (Luke 16:31).

Miracles convince those with a bent to believe. Though he struggled with doubt, Thomas obviously had a desire toward God. As long as God sees that flicker of desire, He'll fan it. If you struggle against doubt, you can take heart from Jesus' kindness to Thomas. He did remind Thomas there would be more joy for those who would believe without such dramatic proof, but He didn't withhold the proof Thomas required to come into solid faith.

And solid faith it apparently became. Thomas was present with the other disciples when Jesus later appeared to them at the Sea of Galilee, and was there again at the Holy Spirit's arrival at Pentecost. And church history records Thomas went on to take the Gospel to India. Perhaps that dogged determination to doubt was baptized by faith into a persistent insistence on belief in the face of massive obstacles.

What to do in the face of doubt? It would have helped

Thomas to be aware of his negative mindset and guard against it. He could also have stayed with the others who believed in Christ, instead of going off alone when things got rough. Together they could have reviewed Christ's miracles, and encouraged their faith with the promises of God.

We can feed our doubts, or we can choose to doubt our doubts and believe what God has for us. As it was for Thomas, the choice is ours.

CHAPTER SEVEN

Jesus and the Man Who Went Out on a Limb

All of Jericho buzzed with the news: the Teacher was coming through town on His way to Jerusalem. Now they would have a chance to see for themselves this one who had created such a stir with His miracles. As His entourage approached, people crowded along the main street, jostling and craning for a look.

Zacchaeus had closed his tax office a bit too late to save himself a good spot along the street, and he chided himself for it. A place on the back row would do no good for a man as short as he. Now he'd either have to miss the parade or find his own way to get a look, for he knew no one would make a place for him. Make room for the hated tax collector? He snorted at the thought of someone even suggesting it. No one ever invited him to join in. He'd gotten even, of course. He had found his own place among the Roman invaders and repaid his neighbors' rejections with his own rejections when they pleaded for leniency against exhorbitant taxes.

Then Zacchaeus spotted the sycamore tree next to the road. Its low, strong branches would do nicely. He settled himself among the green boughs to wait for a glimpse of Jesus. Little did he guess that within a few hours, his encounter with the man coming toward him down the road would change his life.

> Jesus entered Jericho and was passing through. A man was there by the name of Zacchaeus; he was chief tax collector and was wealthy. He wanted to see who Jesus was, but being a short man he could not, because of the crowd. So he ran ahead and climbed a sycamore-fig tree to see Him, since Jesus was coming that way.
>
> When Jesus reached the spot, He looked up and said to him, "Zacchaeus, come down immediately. I must stay at your house today." So he came down at once and welcomed Him gladly.
>
> All the people saw this and began to mutter, "He has gone to be the guest of a 'sinner.'"
>
> But Zacchaeus stood up and said to the Lord, "Look, Lord! Here and now I give half of my possessions to the poor, and if I have cheated anybody out of anything, I will pay back four times the amount."
>
> Jesus said to him, "Today salvation has come to this house, because this man, too, is a son of Abraham. For the Son of Man came to seek and to save what was lost" (Luke 19:1-10).

All people are lost from God, but some of us appear to be more lost than others. Zacchaeus fit this "most lost" category. But Jesus sought him, and brought this outsider into the circle of God's grace.

Jesus Changes Outsiders to Belongers
Zacchaeus was a first-century IRS auditor. Then, as today, tax collectors won no popularity contests. (Have you

ever noticed that if you ask children what they want to be when they grow up, *not one* ever mentions a career with the IRS?) And the Jews seemed to have it much worse than we do when it came to taxes. The temple required a tax to maintain its operation, and King Herod collected taxes to support his lavish building programs. The Roman Empire demanded huge sums from the countries they conquered. All this added up to a tax system in Israel that was oppressive, with tax collectors as the oppressors.

Tax collectors deserved some of the hatred leveled at them. They were, for the most part, an unscrupulous lot, who made their money by overcharging their countrymen, and then skimming from the proceeds before they passed on a share to the Romans. The Romans encouraged this extortion by cleverly setting up their tax collection into a franchise system. For a fee, a Jew could buy the tax franchise for a certain area, agreeing to supply to the Romans a certain amount of tax revenue each year from it. Anything the collector could bring in above this amount, he kept. The franchisee was also free to sublet parts of his territory to others (for a fee, of course!) so they too got in on the take.

Perhaps this is what Zacchaeus had done in Jericho, since he's called a chief taxgatherer. To make matters worse, the tax collectors didn't simply collect too much from everyone alike. They often accepted bribes from the wealthy in exchange for shifting his part of the tax assessment to the poor, some of whom were sold into slavery because they couldn't pay.[1] It's not difficult to understand why Zacchaeus was as detested as he was rich. No one likes a traitor.

During the opening days of a National Football League players' strike, an interviewer asked one of the player representatives how he felt about team members who crossed the picket lines. The hulking football pro hunched his massive shoulders, and answered with a scowl, "I'll say this. When this strike is over, and we meet those guys on the playing field, a lot of us don't intend to go easy on them." I'm sure this is the sentiment many Jews held toward Zaccheus and his colleagues. To have a hated Roman demanding your taxes is one thing, but to have them jerked from you by a fellow Jew is quite another.

No wonder that on the day Jesus came to Jericho, there was no cozy group of friends coaxing Zaccheus to share their spot along the parade route. He was an outsider's outsider, a social leper, reviled by the poor because he was rich, detested by the rich Jews because of how he got his money, and ostracized by the Romans because he was a Jew. Here was a man who belonged nowhere, and to no one. His bank account held all his value as a person; without his money and position, he'd have nothing at all.

What drew Zaccheus to Jesus, strongly enough to cause him to risk ridicule by climbing that sycamore tree? He might have been curious, for a tax collector would have to keep his thumb on stirrings in his district, lest he miss a new source of revenue. Or his curiosity might have been personal. Maybe he wondered about this Jesus, and why He commanded such authority, especially since He lacked the money, prestige, and power base to elicit respect.

Perhaps Zaccheus had heard that Jesus cared about tax collectors. Early in His ministry, Jesus had seen Matthew, a booth attendant who collected taxes from those who used the highways, and called Matthew to follow Him. Later, Matthew threw a party for other tax collectors, so they could encounter Jesus too (see Matt. 9:9-10). Can you imagine the stir this dinner party caused? Author William Coleman comments, "Considering their reputation, it is startling that Jesus would become involved with tax collectors, thus leaving himself wide open to criticism, suspicion, and hostility."² And criticism He received! They said of Him, "Here is a glutton and a drunkard, a friend of tax collectors and 'sinners' " (Luke 7:34). These same Pharisees were perhaps nearby when Jesus met Zacchaeus, because they grumbled, "He has gone to be the guest of a 'sinner' " (Luke 19:7).

If Zacchaeus hoped this friend of sinners might befriend him too, he wasn't disappointed. When Jesus spotted the tax collector, He singled him out. Before the entire crowd, Jesus invited Himself to Zacchaeus' house for lunch. In his life Zacchaeus may never have experienced such warmth and attention from a religious person, and he welcomed Jesus gladly.

Jesus didn't walk over to the sycamore tree to deliver a stinging assessment of the evils of the tax system and those who profited from it. He didn't incite His followers to begin picketing Zacchaeus' office. In fact, He didn't treat Zacchaeus as a tax collector at all; rather, Jesus related to him as a potential friend, a person with needs. And that is, of course, what Zacchaeus was.

Have you ever felt like an outsider? Perhaps in your workplace, or your social circle, or in your church, or even in your family you feel you don't really belong. Maybe you feel unworthy, or guilty, or ostracized for reasons you don't understand. The good news is this: Jesus came to seek the lost. He goes after outsiders, and brings them into friendship with Himself. He told the Laodicean church, "Here I am! I stand at the door and knock. If anyone hears My voice and opens the door, I will go in and eat with him, and he with Me" (Rev. 3:20).

Maybe you've never invited Jesus Christ into your life. Or maybe He is part of your life, but you've not obeyed Him wholeheartedly. Either way, He is seeking you now, and He *wants* to live daily life with you. When He does, He will pull you into the circle of His love, just as He did with Zacchaeus.

Conversion Brings Change

Luke doesn't record what Jesus said to Zacchaeus during their meal together, but he does tell the amazing results. The ruthless tax collector was giving half his wealth to the poor! And with the half he had left, he would repay four times over any money he had taken unjustly.

When God invades a life, changes occur. "If anyone is in Christ, he is a new creation; the old has gone, the new has come!" (2 Cor. 5:17) How appropriate that God's first effect on this man's life would be on his bank account. Materialism and covetousness characterized his life up to this point. He had been willing to climb over others and be hated by everyone around him, just to make a fast buck. Suddenly one-half of everything he had, he gave to the poor. I'm sure the people in the Jericho tax district had no trouble believing something supernatural had happened to Zacchaeus.

A man who lived a few houses from our church had a Zacchaeus-style conversion to Christ. Because his daughter had been injured in an accident, I stopped by his home one Saturday morning to see if I could help. When I shared Christ with him, he understood his need and asked the Lord to be his Saviour. A few months later, at a meeting of the Bible class he was attending, a young woman with Campus Crusade for Christ shared her need for financial support as she ministered to the underprivileged in our city. When she finished, the man came up to me and asked, "Do you think it would be all right if I gave some money to her work, even though I'm not a member of your church?" I assured him that would be fine, so he pulled out his wallet, and stuffed $700 into my hand to give to her. His wife watched the transaction, and with a grin commented, "Now the Lord has his pocketbook."

When the Lord invaded Zacchaeus' pocketbook, the whole town knew his conversion was real. Maybe the changes in us aren't all as dramatic as they were for Zacchaeus, but changes happen when God comes to dwell in our lives. Jesus said the kingdom of God is like yeast in bread dough (Matt. 13:33). Without it, a mix of flour and water and salt and oil is nothing more than a heavy, dead lump. But when yeast invigorates that lump, it rises to be more than it was before. Though it does its work unseen, the yeast eventually affects every particle of the dough, and changes it into something better. When the yeast of the Gospel began to stir in Zacchaeus, the dough fairly exploded from the bread pan!

That very day growth took place that amazed everyone who knew the tax collector. Other changes probably took more time, and even in his financial dealings, Zacchaeus was probably never free from temptations to make money his god. But changes are inevitable when we believe in Christ. We need to look forward to these changes in ourselves and others, and thank God for them so He gets the credit He deserves for what His power can do in us.

Real Belief Means Righting Past Wrongs

It wasn't enough for Zacchaeus to give half his money to the poor. Perhaps he saw this as a way to help release the hold covetousness had on his life. But he understood too that a second act needed to take place. He needed to make things right with individuals he had wronged, by making a fourfold restitution.

Actually the Jewish law required that if one stole, he had to pay the money back, with only a 20 percent penalty, not 300 percent (Lev. 6:5). The only time a fourfold repayment was demanded was in the case of stealing, then killing, another man's sheep (Ex. 22:1). Maybe Zacchaeus knew the law so vaguely he wasn't clear on what it required. But it's possible too that he was so grateful to God for forgiving and accepting him, that only a fourfold repayment could express his appreciation and clear his sense of guilt.

Paul gave a good guideline when he said, "I strive always to keep my conscience clear before God and man" (Acts 24:16). Admitting our sin to God is vital to clear communication between us, but it's also important we keep things clear with people as well. Where we have wronged others, we need to make it straight.

Some years ago, a lady applied to join our church who had had a history of shoplifting. When she met with the church officials, she admitted she had stolen a number of times in the past year, before becoming a Christian that August. "In September," she said, "I shoplifted one more time, and I was caught in a very foolish way." She felt that through her arrest God was saying, "You are My child now, so stop this stealing!" And she did.

The church officials decided that the act of shoplifting was much less an issue than her sorrow for her sin. Because of her obvious repentance, they decided her arrest wouldn't affect her church membership. I told her of our decision, but then I asked, "Did it ever occur to you to go back to the places you robbed and make restitution?" She admitted she'd not thought of it, and we left it at that.

But a couple of weeks later, she called to tell me she wanted to set things right, and asked if I'd go with her. We met with the manager of each of the four stores where she'd shoplifted. The woman was a member of my congregation, I explained, and wanted to make restitution for things she had wrongfully taken from the store. She then presented a list of the items, and we asked she be allowed to pay for them with interest, as if she'd bought them on credit.

If you think these encounters were easy, you've never had to say "I was wrong." Besides the personal embarrassment it cost the woman, the money she owed was significant. The bill for one store alone ran nearly $800. Then, of course, there was always the question of prosecution. She wasn't admitting to a silly mistake or a slip of the tongue; she was confessing to a crime. Her courage in offering restitution was a genuine act of faith.

None of the managers prosecuted. In fact, they were so overwhelmed with her courage in coming to them that some even had tears in their eyes. But most importantly, after it was done, the woman said to me, "I feel so clean." This is the clear conscience Paul talked about, and to possess it is a freeing experience indeed.

Is there anything for which you need to make restitution? Or anyone from whom you need to seek forgiveness? When you ask God to play back the video of your life to date, what do you see? Is He pointing out to you any wrongs you've not admitted to Him? If so, confess your sin, and experience the joy of His forgiveness. Then check the video again. Are there things you need to make right with others? The Lord's words through Solomon still stand in good stead today. "He who conceals his sins does not prosper, but whoever confesses and renounces them finds mercy" (Prov. 28:13).

After Zacchaeus paid back the money he had wrongfully taken, he was financially poorer. Considering how unscrupulous most tax collectors were, we might wonder if Zacchaeus came away from his commitment with anything left at all! But he could walk down the street and look everyone he met in the eye, with a conscience clear that he had done all he could to right his past wrongs. And he could certainly trust that his new Master would supply all he needed to live this life of obedience to which he had been called. When Zacchaeus obeyed, it became God's responsibility to care for him in the consequences of his obedience.

Some wrongs can't be completely righted. How could Paul have made adequate restitution to those Christians he had persecuted? There was no way to undo the past. For some wrongs, we can do no more than go to those we've hurt, and seek their forgiveness. Sometimes that's not even possible. Or we ask for forgiveness, and the wounded ones refuse to grant it. When that happens, we can still know peace, because God's requirement is, "Be careful to do what is right in the eyes of everybody. If it is possible, as far as it depends on you, live at peace with everyone" (Rom. 12:17-18). If we've done all we can to make restitution, the rest is up to God. We're not responsible for the responses of others to our obedience.

There are no words in our language harder to say than, "I was wrong. Please forgive me." But for his obedience, Zacchaeus received a joyful commendation from Christ. "Today salvation has come to this house, because this man too is a son of Abraham" (Luke 19:9). The outsider now belonged. The man out on a limb came to safety. Because of his faith, God has accepted this outcast for all eternity. Coming to faith and making restitution for our wrongs may cost us some prestige and relationships. But the cost is slight compared to gaining Christ.

NOTES

1. William L. Coleman, *Today's Handbook of Bible Times and Customs* (Minneapolis: Bethany House Publishers, 1984), pp. 186-187.

2. Ibid., p. 187.

CHAPTER EIGHT

Jesus and the Woman Who Didn't Miss the Boat

When the Baptist theologian A.H. Strong looked for an illustration to bring home how faith in Christ grows, he chose this one: '

A man alone on an island notices the water surrounding his place of safety is beginning to rise a bit. He notices also a little boat anchored nearby. Though he considers the information about the water's level, and the boat's existence interesting, neither seems terribly important to him, so he mentally files them away and goes about his business. This is the *knowledge* stage of coming to solid faith.[1]

The water continues to rise. Now the man looks at the information available to him differently. He inspects the boat and decides it looks solid enough to keep him afloat, should the situation worsen. He could trust himself to the boat and probably be in good stead. Now he's gone beyond simple knowledge, to the point of *assent;* he believes the boat can save him, if need be.

But then water inundates the last bit of solid ground, and our friend climbs into the boat, depending on it to deliver him from drowning. As our friend commits himself to the boat, this act of *trust* marks the arrival of real faith.

On His way to heal a religious ruler's daughter, Jesus encountered a woman who had sense enough—and faith enough—not to miss the boat. She *knew* of Jesus; stories of His power had drawn her to *assent* that He could heal. Now she left the security of anonymity and reached out to Him with an act of *trust*, and heard Him say, "Daughter, your faith has healed you."

A large crowd followed and pressed around Him. And a woman was there who had been subject to bleeding for twelve years. She had suffered a great deal under the care of many doctors and had spent all she had, yet instead of getting better she grew worse. When she heard about Jesus, she came up behind Him in the crowd and touched His cloak, because she thought, "If I just touch His clothes, I will be healed." Immediately her bleeding stopped and she felt in her body that she was freed from her suffering.

At once Jesus realized that power had gone out from Him. He turned around in the crowd and asked, "Who touched My clothes?"

"You see the people crowding against You," His disciples answered, "and yet You can ask, 'Who touched Me?' "

But Jesus kept looking around to see who had done it. Then the woman, knowing what had happened to her, came and fell at His feet and, trembling with fear, told Him the whole truth. He said to her, "Daughter, your faith has healed you. Go in peace and be freed from your suffering" (Mark 5:24b-34).

No Situation Is Ever Impossible with Christ

Sometimes we hear the verdict "impossible" pronounced over our problem, and we give up.

This woman came to Jesus with a problem the experts of her day had pronounced unsolvable. Her damaged body was irreparable, her illness irreversible. Luke, himself a medical doctor, made this clear in his description of the woman. "No one could heal her," he reported. Mark points out that the incurable nature of her illness was agreed upon by a number of medical experts. "She had suffered a great deal under the care of *many* doctors and had spent all she had, yet instead of getting better, she grew worse." (The Bible is not without humor. It is interesting to note that in his account, Dr. Luke omits any references to the woman's physicians taking all her money without delivering any relief. A professional courtesy to his colleagues, perhaps?)

The point is, this woman had been hemorrhaging for twelve years and had exhausted all her financial and medical resources in the search for a cure that did not appear to exist. Had you been her physician, or her friend, or her pastor, what would you have advised?

Unfortunately, I fear that many of us far too quickly accept some expert's "impossible" verdict as the final word. When an accountant looks over our debts and tells us there is no way out but bankruptcy, we meekly accept our fate. When our spouse informs us there's no hope for the marriage, and divorce is the only way, we pack our suitcases and look for the nearest chapter of Parents without Partners. When a friend says he or she has been hurt too many times, and there's no hope for release from the bitterness, we sigh weakly and give our friend up to misery. When a relative's medical test reveals cancer, we start deciding what we'll wear to the funeral.

"But with God, *all things are possible!*"

All things? Rescue from financial disaster? Rebirth of married love? Forgiveness and healing for wounds of the past? Cures for incurable diseases?

In my deepest spirit, I know the answer is a resounding yes. The God who can start with nothing more than darkness and speak a world into existence, who can instantaneously split a sea in half so 2 million people can walk through it; who can reverse the sun in its course across the sky, who can walk on water, and restore a withered hand, and command blindness to be gone, and call the dead back to life—this God knows no impossibilities.

But I have to be honest. Even though I've committed my life to this God of the Impossible, sometimes I respond to life's crises with what appears to be a "reluctant realism." I blithely accept statistical probabilities, or expert opinion, or past experience as being conclusive, rather than considering what God can do. I sometimes fear that if this woman had been in my congregation, I might have been tempted to counsel her, "Look. You've had this disease for twelve years—and all the studies say every year you have it, the chances of a cure get less. And you seem to be getting worse, not better. And the people God has provided to help us fight disease don't see any hope for you. Maybe you better just accept this illness as your cross to bear and learn to rejoice in suffering."

Isn't it fortunate this woman didn't get such advice? She'd have missed out on being healed because her counselor forgot we're involved with a God who does the impossible.

Of course I'm not so naive as to believe it's *always* God's plan to remove illness and avert defeat. If that were so, none of us would ever die! Jesus would have died on the cross only because He didn't have enough faith to see God deliver Him. And God's Word would be in error when it records God telling Paul that He wanted to use

Paul's "thorn in the flesh" for God's glory, rather than heal it (2 Cor. 12:9).

But I do wonder if God might not do many more miracles in our midst if we could let go and let Him tackle more of the things we call impossible. After all, what does "impossible" really mean? To most of us, it means things *we've* never seen or heard of happening. But think back a few hundred years. To Christians of those times, it surely seemed impossible that smallpox could be virtually eliminated from the world, or that man could walk on the moon. These things seemed impossible, because people had never seen them done. Today we would laugh at those who consider these feats impossible.

This propensity toward accepting as possible only what we see is why we so badly need to be reminded of stories like that of this ill woman. That's one reason why it's so important we read the Bible. "For everything that was written in the past was written to teach us, so that through endurance and the encouragement of the Scriptures we might have hope" (Rom. 15:4).

The Bible bubbles over with stories of the impossible becoming reality as God intervenes. Children defeat giants, city walls crumble at a trumpet blast, and lame men dance. We need to rehearse these stories of faith victories to each other, so that we give God the room He needs to make the impossible possible for us.

A woman in our congregation went to the stories of Hannah and Sarah when she was told by her doctors she couldn't have children. She realized both these women received the same dire prognosis she did, yet Hannah gave birth to Samuel and six other children, and Sarah became the mother of Isaac. God used these accounts to stir her faith that she also might bear a child. Today this woman has gladly joined Hannah and Sarah on the list of barren women who went on to give birth.

We need to rehearse the present-day miracles of God to each other too. Jesus saw to it that the woman told the crowd how He had healed her. It was *after* she told her story she heard Jesus' firm assurance: "Daughter, your faith has healed you. Go in peace and be freed from your suffering." There seems to be a blessing of assurance that comes to us when God works, and we verbally affirm it. In Romans 10:9-10 we read this about salvation: "If you confess with your mouth, 'Jesus is Lord,' and believe in your heart that God raised Him from the dead, you will be saved. For it is with your heart that you believe and are justified, and it is with your mouth that you confess and are saved."

Jesus had already healed this woman's bleeding before she told her story, and she knew the healing had taken place. "Her bleeding stopped and she felt in her body that she was freed from her suffering," Mark reports. Giving verbal testimony to her healing didn't cause her illness to flee; Jesus had already done that. But it may have given her assurance and confidence when she returned home and people said, "This is probably just some temporary remission; the doctors all said you'd never get well."

When the Book of Revelation records the great accuser, Satan, hurled out of heaven, it gives this clue to his defeat. "They overcome him by the blood of the Lamb, and by the word of their testimony" (Rev. 12:11). The verbal witness of those fighting against Satan seems to have authority to break his power, just as Christ's shed blood does. Perhaps in giving this woman opportunity to witness to her healing, Jesus knew Satan's power to accuse and harass her growing faith was stymied.

In any case, telling what God has done certainly seems to confirm and energize our faith. We need to be as careful to circulate the *answers* we see to our prayers, as we are to tell others of our *requests*. We need to work as hard at reminding each other of times He *did* heal, and *did* restore a marriage, and *did* rescue from failure, as we are to tell of times He didn't.

It also helps to remind each other of what God has promised to do. A few years ago, our church decided together to trust God for a significant sum of money to meet a need we had. As churches often do, we asked for pledges from the congregation, but the initial amount pledged fell far short of our goal. When we had less than a month before the money had to be raised, the chairman of the campaign and I decided to start praying together about the need. He would stop by my office every day after work, and we'd greet each other with a standard set of questions. "How much came in today?" "How much do we still have to go?" "How many in the congregation still haven't made a commitment?"

These questions got us nowhere, because when we focused on the congregation, my faith would go to zero. It was obvious we'd never make the goal.

But then we'd take our eyes off the congregation and get out the Bible. "If you ask anything according to My will, I will do it." "He is able to do exceeding abundantly above all that we can ask or think."

As we'd read those promises, my faith would go up! But when we would wander off and talk about the congregation again, I could feel my faith sink. And as we returned to Scripture, up it would go again. I think if I had realized earlier I needed to stop relying on the congregation and rely only on what God had promised, my bobbing faith could have stabilized more quickly. Focusing on His promises can help our faith grow. (We did meet our financial goal, by the way, but as He often does, God provided in an unusual way.)

Because our God *is* God, no situation is ever really

impossible. Let's stop accepting others' assessment of what's "realistic" to expect, and let this woman's example challenge us to confront an impossible diagnosis with faith. His help may result in the freedom from pain we expect, or it may take the form of freedom *in* the pain. In his book, *You Gotta Keep Dancin'!* (David C. Cook), Tim Hansel relates how his healing came in this form.

> For years people have asked me, "Haven't you prayed to the Lord for healing?"
>
> My obvious answer: "Of course."
>
> "Why do you think He hasn't healed you?"
>
> "He has."
>
> "But I thought you were still in pain."
>
> "I am."
>
> "I don't understand."
>
> "I have prayed hundreds, if not thousands, of times for the Lord to heal me—and He finally *healed me of the need to be healed*." I had discovered a peace inside the pain.
>
> I finally came to the realization that if the Lord could use this body better the way it is, then that's the way it should be. I'm quite sure that I would be a different person, were it not for my accident. For the past ten years, I've had the opportunity to be on the steepest learning curve in my whole life. I feel like I've gotten a Ph.D. in living.

God met and graced Tim Hansel with the same power He gave to the hemorrhaging woman. Both saw His touch set them free of the oppression of their suffering, because they trusted Him to do the impossible.

Jesus, Not Holy Fringe, Heals

This woman came to Jesus with one idea clearly in mind:

if she could touch His clothing, she would be healed. Where she got this idea, Scripture doesn't say, but a look at the history of the times may give us some clues. First-century rabbis often doubled as physicians, since properly licensed doctors weren't nearly as numerous as were the sick. So for this woman to look to a religious teacher for medical help, especially when physicians had done so little for her, wouldn't have been outlandish.

In several Bible translations, the phrase "His cloak" is explained as "the hem of His garment" or "the fringe of His cloak." To Jews of the day, this fringe that adorned the edge of the outer garment was far more than simply decorative. God commanded they put it there. Back in the Book of Numbers, when God was setting down the pattern of life for His people, He instructed them thusly, "Throughout the generations to come you are to make tassels on the corners of your garments, with a blue cord on each tassel. You will have these tassels to look at and so you will remember all the commands of the Lord, that you may obey them" (Num. 15:38-39). So this fringe had special spiritual significance, so much so that the Pharisees adorned their cloaks with fringe much wider than everyone else's to emphasize how much their spirituality exceeded that of all others.

Perhaps these factors gave her the faith and the incentive she needed to elbow her way through a crushing crowd and reach out to Jesus. And just what she expected happened! When her fingers touched the fringe on Christ's coat, her bleeding stopped.

Word of what happened obviously spread, because just one chapter later, in Mark 6, this observation is made. "Everywhere He [Jesus] went—into villages, towns or countryside—they placed the sick in the marketplaces. They begged Him to let them touch even the edge of His cloak" (Mark 6:56). This woman's success must have made an impact, because the idea of touching Jesus' cloak is never recorded in the Gospels before her encounter with Christ, but after she received healing, many sought to grab onto that fringe, and they too were cured.

Was this woman healed because of special power in the fringe on Jesus' coat? Of course not! Jesus made it clear that her *faith* had made her well. Touching His garment simply provided a means to help focus her faith, but her faith was in Him and He healed in response to her faith.

But perhaps some confused this simple contact point for her faith with the Source of her healing. Don't you suppose that after her story got out, sales of cloak-fringe boomed? I'll bet the value of fringe manufacturing stock skyrocketed, and fringe companies were taking orders faster than they could process them! The disciples were probably all tempted to change the fringe on their cloaks to match the exact size, color, and design of Christ's. Religious thinkers likely sat around discussing what kind of fringe might be most effective to cure what diseases. If those around Jesus were at all like us, many thought Jesus' fringe, not the woman's faith in Christ, was the source for her healing.

When Paul, Apollos, and Cephas ministered to the church at Corinth, God's power moved through them with supernatural effects. When God used these men as channels of His power, the Corinthians began to worship *them*. Paul was horrified! "What, after all, is Apollos? And what is Paul? Only servants through whom you came to believe—as *the Lord* assigned to each his task . . . you are *God's* field, *God's* building. . . . Don't you know that you yourselves are *God's* temple and that *God's* Spirit lives in you?" (1 Cor. 3:5, 9, 16, italics added) Paul knew well that the work was only God's and that if these Corinthians came to trust the Healer's fringe instead of the Healer Himself, their faith was doomed to die.

All of us have some medium God used to help us trust Him. Perhaps it was some special Bible study, or a seminar, or a television program, or some local church! God's power moved through them to us in an electric way, and our lives have never been the same. If we feel love, respect, and appreciation for them, that's wonderful. Paul expected those to whom he ministered to love him in return. But we do want to be careful we don't begin believing these people or events were ever *essential* for our healing, to the point of giving them the worship that belongs only to God. He may need to allow them to disappoint us, so it's clear they're only channels of His life, not the Source of life itself.

How God Helps Us Grow in Faith
The Scripture doesn't tell us how this woman came into such remarkable faith. And when His disciples asked Him to increase their faith, Jesus' answer wouldn't make a very good three-point sermon outline. Have faith like a mustard seed, He told them, and this mulberry tree will obey you when you tell it to uproot and plant itself in the ocean (Luke 17:6). Another time he told them faith like a mustard seed can move a mountain (Matt. 17:20).

Mustard seeds aren't a part of our everyday lives, as they were in the lives of Jesus' hearers, so it's important to see what Jesus thought significant about them to see why He chose this particular object to explain how faith can grow. Every other time mustard seeds are mentioned in the Gospels, the same point about them is always made. They are the smallest of seeds, yet they grow up to very large trees that provide good shelter. Jesus seems to be saying that the amount of our faith isn't the issue; a small faith can produce a great work that greatly benefits others. The *quantity* of our faith seems to matter less than the *quality*.

On what does the quality of our faith depend? *Who* we believe in matters and *what we do with the faith we have.* This hemorrhaging woman believed *Christ* would be the source of her healing, and she *came to Him* to obtain a cure. A huge faith in anything other than Christ would not have healed her. Likewise, a general, sentimental belief in Christ without coming to Him for help in her need wouldn't have healed her, either.

If we trust Christ, and do what we can with the faith we have, God will help us believe. I draw courage from the desperate father who brought his demon-possessed son to Jesus. He had no ringing faith like the hemorrhaging woman's. The best he could do was plead, " 'If You can do anything, take pity on us and help us!' 'If You can?' said Jesus. 'Everything is possible for him who believes.' Immediately the boy's father exclaimed, 'I do believe; help me overcome my unbelief ' " (Mark 9:22-23). And Jesus healed his son.

Some of us come to faith by striding confidently over to the boat and climbing in; others of us struggle to the craft, take a deep breath, and tumble in. But as long as we trust ourselves to Christ, we'll join the hemorrhaging woman in not missing the boat and, as she did, we'll see God work on our behalf.

NOTES

1. A.H. Strong, *Systematic Theology* (Philadelphia: Judson Press, 1947), p. 839.

CHAPTER NINE

Jesus and the Gambling Widow

Have you heard the one about the three ministers comparing notes on how they determined how much of their income to give to God?

"I draw a circle around myself, and throw my money up in the air," the youth minister explained. "All the money that lands inside the circle belongs to me, and everything outside the circle goes to the Lord."

"My system is a little different," the music minister said. "I draw a circle around myself too, but when I throw my bills in the air, I give the Lord everything inside the circle, and keep all that falls outside for myself."

The senior minister looked at the two reprovingly. "I'm surprised at your spiritual immaturity," he clucked. "I always *pray* that the Lord will get His share. Then I throw my money in the air, and everything the Lord wants, He takes. I keep the rest."

Like this minister, we're adept at hiding behind a front of pseudo spirituality to protect ourselves from having to jump into the risky business of giving by faith. For us, faith has little to do with gambling. We relegate the high-stakes gamblers to Las Vegas, or Wall Street. But these high rollers could learn a thing or two about taking risks from a poor, anonymous widow who lived in Judea nearly 2,000 years ago. When she gave, she gambled all she had by faith, and won the praise of the Son of God.

Jesus sat down opposite the place where the offerings were put and watched the crowd putting their money into the temple treasury. Many rich people threw in large amounts. But a poor widow came and put in two very small copper coins, worth only a fraction of a penny.

Calling His disciples to Him, Jesus said, "I tell you the truth, this poor widow has put more into the treasury than all the others. They all gave out of their wealth; but she, out of her poverty, put in everything—all she had to live on" (Mark 12:41-44).

Our Giving Matters to God

Imagine, if you will, the conversations of Eisenhower and his generals the week before D Day. As they poured over maps, and checked munitions supplies, they only had time to consider those things that would insure success for their approaching attempt to turn the fate of the war. I doubt they spent much time discussing how to improve the flavor of the C rations, or whether or not Bob Hope was scheduled for a Christmas show in England that year.

Listen in on the pregame pep talk as an NFL coach addresses his roomful of hulking heroes-to-be just before they charge onto the field of Superbowl XXV. Is he discussing dance steps for their next team video, or taking a vote on whether or not the front office ought to fire the guy who books their hotels for road games? Hardly. A wise coach uses those final minutes to talk over essentials and nothing else.

The incident we're discussing, the widow's generous gift, took place just before the Lord's D Day on the cross. Jesus had entered Jerusalem triumphantly, and now during these fragile days between that moment of glory and the suffering at Calvary, we see Him taking His last strokes in the lives of those who would carry on His mission.

This particular day, perhaps Tuesday of Holy Week, had been a demanding one. From the moment Jesus arrived in Jerusalem, His enemies had been circling Him like a pack of hungry wolves looking for the most vulnerable spot to begin tearing Him apart. He would end this grueling day with a long, prophetic session explaining to His disciples what to expect in the final days of earth's history. The day held all the intensity and drama you would expect as the leader of a world-changing movement prepared to leave His closest followers. He reinforced the fundamental truths that would keep them true to Him through the nightmare ahead and beyond.

But quietly sandwiched into the middle of this day, Scripture records a fascinating interlude. Before leaving the temple, Jesus sat down opposite the place where the offerings were being collected to watch people give their gifts. He took careful note of who came and how much they gave.

Suppose when they were taking up the offering at your church, the minister stepped out from behind the podium and followed the ushers up and down each aisle, peering intently down the rows to catch just how much each parishioner put in the plate. That's in essence what Jesus did. Why did He take time out from essentials for these moments of holy meddling? I think it was because He knew that what we do with our possessions *is* a matter of genuine urgency. Giving is mentioned over 300 times in the New Testament. It's one of the most talked about subjects, running neck-and-neck with the Second Coming. Why does God care so much about how we give?

First, our giving shows how much we *love* God. Jesus explained, "Where your treasure is, there your heart will be also" (Matt. 6:21).

In his lively book *God Can Make It Happen* (Victor Books), author Russ Johnston tells of a teacher who understood this principle very well. He relates:

> An economics professor at Iowa State University who wanted to interest his students in Wall Street came up with the perfect way to do it. He didn't assign them a term paper on it, nor ask them to give reports, nor threaten them with a test. He simply gave them $1,000 and let them invest it. He almost needed a referee before class every day to keep order as the students fought over who was to read the *Wall Street Journal* first to see how the stock was doing.

We love the things our money is invested in, and we invest our money in the things we love. If we're passionate about God and His work, our checkbook will show it.

Second, our giving reveals how much we *know* God. The Apostle John explained, "This is how we know what love is: Jesus Christ laid down His life for us. And we ought to lay down our lives for our brothers. If anyone has material possessions and sees his brother in need but has no pity on him, how can the love of God be in him?" (1 John 3:16-17) If we truly understand God's generous nature and His grace to us, we'll demonstrate that same grace toward those around us who need it.

A while back I got a call from an elderly gentleman who wanted to know about Christ. His niece had written him about her recent conversion, and though he didn't understand all she'd said, she had piqued his interest. We made an appointment to meet, and in that first conversation, he gave his life to the Saviour.

About a month later, this man told me about a collection some people in his area were taking for a little girl suffering with leukemia. "I gave a fair amount," he told me, "but I just realized it really didn't hurt me to give. I don't think I'm even going to miss the money, so I don't think I gave enough."

Grace had taken root in this new believer! His desire to give sacrificially showed me he understood Christ had richly given to him.

Third, by our giving, we show how much we *trust* God. A rich, young ruler came to Jesus to ask the way to eternal life. "I've kept all the commandments," the young man insisted.

"One thing you lack," Jesus told the young man. "Go, sell everything you have and give to the poor, and you will have treasure in heaven. Then come, follow Me" (Mark 10:21).

Many other things this young man would have done gladly to earn eternal life. Perhaps he might have even given a large part of his goods to the poor. But all? With this one demand, Jesus cut straight to the heart of his security, confidence, and pride. His wealth was his identity and his life, so Jesus demanded that he forsake it to win life eternal.

Have you noticed that Jesus has the most irritating habit of trouncing over our spiritual rhetoric and holy baloney to hit on the one issue that determines whether or not we're willing to be totally His? "I want eternal life, Lord," this young man decided, "but not at the expense of my fortune." Others say, "I'd be Yours, Lord, but not if it means giving up this relationship I cherish." "Yes, I'll follow You, Lord, anywhere but. . . ." "Give up my profession for You, Lord? You know I can't. . . ."

For Abraham, the call to commitment came when the Lord told him to slay his only son Isaac. With us, it may be giving up someone we love, so we can say with the psalmist, "There is none on earth I desire more than Thee" (Ps. 73:25, KJV). It may be some prized possession or a professional dream. What would hurt you too much to give up? What are you grasping? It isn't what *we have;* it's what *has us* that matters to God. Our giving can be a way to test whether or not faith actually controls our hearts.

God Honors Those Whose Giving Costs Them the Most

The widow Jesus observed gave barely a penny—a small gift by everyone's definition. But at the same time, it was the largest gift given, because it was 100 percent of what she had. Who else at the temple that day had even come close to such generosity—and such faith?

I wonder if this gutsy widow and her generosity served to spark the churches in Macedonia to give when it hurt? "Out of the most severe trial," Paul reports, "their over-flowing joy and their extreme poverty welled up in rich generosity. For I testify that they gave as much as they were able, and even beyond their ability. Entirely on their own, they urgently pleaded with us for the privilege of sharing in this service to the saints" (2 Cor. 8:2-4).

Cheerful givers? These believers lead the pack. Theirs was no reluctant digging into a trouser pocket for a wallet they hoped would be empty so they'd have an excuse not to give. These Christians begged for the privilege of giv-ing. They fought for the honor, just as we struggle to get our kids into the Talented and Gifted Program at school or politic to get to sing the solo in the choir's Christmas cantata.

The Macedonians were giving from poverty, giving the

last that they had. This was risky giving, as risky as sign-
ing a contract without the terms filled in, or diving off a
diving board without first being sure the pool is filled
with water. Since they gave from poverty, they could face
ruin unless God's promises to supply their needs were
true. Their faith was a holy risk, a godly gamble. They
risked starving themselves, or not having enough to care
for those they loved. But God's best praise goes to those
whose giving leaves them nothing to depend on but
Himself.

Are you in poverty? Perhaps, like this widow, your situation is hilariously impossible. She couldn't live on a mere
penny, just as you can't possibly make it on the resources
you have. Some will encourage you to plead, "I'm so poor
I have nothing to give." But don't listen to them! Don't
wait until you think you have "enough" to be able to give.
Giving isn't an issue of convenience; it's a matter of faith.
Whatever keeps you from giving when you're poor, will
also keep you from giving when you're rich. Jesus said,
"Whoever can be trusted with very little can also be trusted with much, and whoever is dishonest with very little
will also be dishonest with much" (Luke 16:10).

Just because people have an abundance of money, it
doesn't necessarily follow they'll give to God. A million-
aire I know spent nearly our whole dinner hour together
explaining to me why it was utterly impossible for him to
give 10 percent of his money to the Lord. "It's all these
investments," he complained. "They have my money all
tied up, so with such a small cash flow, there's just no
money free to give." I wish he could have moaned over
his predicament to this Judean widow, who in the original
Greek was described as "the poorest of the poor." She
teaches us that we always have something to give, no matter how poor we appear to be. And the gifts that cost us
the most bring the most pleasure to God.

A pastor in Iowa recalled how in his days at Asbury Seminary he and his wife decided they simply had to stop giving. His wife had excellent secretarial skills, so they planned that as soon as they hit Kentucky, she'd land a super job, and they'd have the money they needed to live on and care for their two small children during their years in school. But the job didn't materialize. She wound up in a factory sewing dresses for barely enough wages to even pay the rent and feed them, so giving seemed out of the question. Besides, the man reasoned, he was studying for the ministry. He was giving time and intellect to God. If anyone was justified in not giving his money, surely it would be a seminary student!

But after a year of barely scraping by, this young man's church challenged him to give, even from his poverty. "At first I was offended," the man recalled. "I thought they had a lot of nerve asking *me* to give when I was already doing so much for the Lord, and had so little income as a result. But I finally gave in and pledged we'd begin giving a small amount every week."

Two things happened. First, the seminary student's feelings about himself began to change. "When you feel too poor to give, you really feel poor," he laughed, "and when we began giving, even though the amount was paltry, I began to experience a greater personal confidence and self-respect." Not long after, his wife was offered an excellent secretarial job in the College of Nursing at the University of Kentucky Medical Center, a job which paid nearly twice what she was earning before.

"We don't think it was coincidental that job came when it did," the pastor reflected. "I think now that if we'd been quicker to give from our poverty, God would have been free to give us that better job earlier. We learned from that experience that it's not a matter of being able to afford to give. We simply can't afford *not* to give!"

Maybe some resource other than money seems to be lacking in your life. Are you time-poor, unable to cram one more activity into your jam-packed schedule? Give some of your precious moments to God, perhaps to listen to someone who is hurting, or to relax when He decides to interrupt your schedule. Are you love-poor, fearful of losing the few people in your life who seem to really care for you? Maybe you need to share some of their love or time with others, by encouraging your spouse to help with a church painting weekend, or being glad when your best friend volunteers to lead a Bible study on the evening you usually get together. Like our widow of Judea, you're never too poor to give! She had a right to be receiving from the temple funds, but she was contributing to them instead. The one in need gave—and won Jesus' praise.

Maybe your spiritual gift is a small gift. You can't preach to great multitudes, or evangelize thousands, or heal the masses. The widow could have looked at the size of the rich men's gifts, and wondered, "What's the use? What good can my pittance do to further God's work? Now, if I could only give as they do. . . ." But fortunately she didn't. She took the small gift she had, offered it freely, and was singled out for Jesus' praise. Bring your small gift without apology, and offer it to God. He'll use it to further His work and minister to His children, just as He did with this woman's penny. And you'll bring delight to Him, just as the widow did.

A Gamble on God Makes a Sure Bet

You're no gambler if the horse you put money on can't lose. And our widow wasn't actually a gambler at all when she gave all she had to God. Some probably shook their heads, called her foolish, and predicted she would starve, but she had access to inside information they didn't. She knew God had committed Himself to care for widows. And she knew of promises God had made like, "Bring the whole tithe into the storehouse . . . and see if I will not throw open the floodgates of heaven and pour out so much blessing that you will not have room enough for it" (Mal. 3:10).

What did the widow receive for the gift she gave? For one thing, she gained lasting prominence. Think of the people who've spent millions building monuments, or establishing positions of power, in an attempt to keep their memory alive after they've died. Two thousand years after her death, this woman is still known around the world, yet this lasting reputation cost her less than a penny.

She also received the joy that comes with being a contributor to God's work. And she received praise from Jesus Himself. During His last week on earth, she had the privilege of blessing Jesus, all by doing nothing more than giving what she had. Scripture doesn't record what happened to her materially after this episode, but I believe in the same promises she did. Therefore, I believe God supplied all her needs, both to care for her, and so she could continue to enjoy the privilege of giving to others.

When a man I know became a Christian, he felt an immediate desire to want to use his money for the good of Christ's kingdom. He'd heard of the concept of giving 10 percent of your income to the Lord's work, but since he made a good income, he felt 10 percent wasn't enough, so he began giving 20 percent. This act surprised him more than anyone, since the year before his conversion he'd given his church only $250 total—a smaller amount than he'd spent on whiskey that same year.

After a year of this 20 percent giving, this man's income increased to $30,000, and he wanted his giving to increase as well. About that time, he read the biblical account of Zacchaeus believing in Christ. The tax collector gave half of everything he had, and my friend wondered if he should do the same. After prayer and conferring with his wife, he believed God was encouraging him to give to the Lord's work 20 percent of everything he earned up to $30,000, but he was to give 50 percent of everything over $30,000.

He reported, "During my first three years as a Christian I was able to return to the Lord approximately $20,000—a figure I would have choked on four years ago." He reveled in the pleasure of giving back to God who had given to him so generously. But a surprise awaited him when he made up a year-end financial statement. "I realized my net worth had increased during those three years by over $200,000—more than ten times the amount I had returned to the Lord." When we give to God, He is no one's debtor. He promises to care for us, and often does it far more generously than we could have imagined.

Of course, God's care doesn't always come to us in neat, six-figure packages. Ricky, one of our church members, began the adventure of giving from a position more like the widow's poverty. He was so badly in debt that panic calls from his wife had become commonplace. "The man from the power company is here and is going to cut off the power," she'd tell him. Another day it would be the phone company disconnecting services because of unpaid bills. In the midst of this mess, Ricky heard a challenge on giving, and decided he had to begin giving. But when he did, there was no instant rescue. Instead, things he'd never thought of went wrong. The clothes dryer gave out, their furnace quit working, and on it went. Ricky was tempted to rescind on his commitment to give to God.

But he remembered he hadn't started giving in an attempt to buy God's blessing, so he wouldn't quit just because material blessing didn't seem to be forthcoming. The next month, Ricky made the largest sale in his career, and he caught up with his debts. He rejoiced in God's kindness, but he rejoiced more that God had helped him give when it didn't appear that a glorious rescue was on the way.

We'll earn *God's* praise if, like the poor widow, we give what we can't afford to part with. As we do, we'll be entering into the risky, wonderful venture of trusting a God who cannot fail.

CHAPTER TEN

Jesus and the Man Born Blind

Perhaps on some radio station that plays "Golden Old-ies," you've heard a singer croon, "If I ruled the world, every day would be the first day of spring." These lyrics should pique the interest of Christians, because we be-long to the One who, in fact, does rule the world. But He dictates that the first day of spring comes only once a year. The other 364 days consist of a mix of winter storms and blue Mondays, with some Fourth of Julys and Christmas Eves thrown in here and there.

We believe God is loving, kind, and only does good; yet He allows pain and suffering into this Eden He created, even though He has the power to obliterate it. Sooner or later, even the most faithful of us ask why.

I am not audacious enough to claim that the next few pages will solve the questions of the ages about why hu-manity suffers. But I do believe that in His interaction with a blind man, Jesus provided some insights that will help us when we encounter pain.

As He went along, [Jesus] saw a man blind from

birth. His disciples asked Him, "Rabbi, who sinned, this man or his parents, that he was born blind?"

"Neither this man nor his parents sinned," said Jesus, "but this happened so that the work of God might be displayed in his life. As long as it is day, we must do the work of Him who sent Me. Night is coming, when no one can work. While I am in the world, I am the light of the world."

Having said this, He spit on the ground, made some mud with the saliva, and put it on the man's eyes. "Go," He told him, "wash in the pool of Siloam" (this word means Sent). So the man went and washed, and came home seeing.

• • • • • • • • • • •

Jesus heard that [the Pharisees] had thrown [the blind man] out, and when He found him, He said, "Do you believe in the Son of Man?"

"Who is He, sir?" the man asked. "Tell me so that I may believe in Him."

Jesus said, "You have now seen Him; in fact, He is the one speaking with you."

Then the man said, "Lord, I believe," and he worshiped Him (John 9:1-7, 35-38).

Suffering Isn't Easy to Explain

This drama of suffering and wholeness opens where we most usually begin when we encounter pain. The disciples spotted a man, blind from birth, and asked, "Why, Lord?"

To the disciples, this was a question that could have only one of two answers. They believed suffering was a punishment for sin, as did most of the religious community of the day. Of course this man was born blind, so he couldn't be enduring punishment for his own sin, but

JESUS AND THE MAN BORN BLIND / 111

someone's sin had to cause the malady. So, the disciples wondered if his parents were at fault. They gave Jesus two choices and awaited His reply.

Today, many still believe sin causes suffering, and Scripture teaches it certainly does. Adam and Eve disobeyed God and were banished from the Garden of Eden to bear pain in childbirth and struggle in making a living. Cain killed his brother Abel, and a number of painful punishments followed. The Children of Israel refused to believe God and had to die in the wilderness as a result. After Jesus healed a lame man, He warned him, "See, you are well again. Stop sinning or something worse may happen to you" (John 5:14). In the days of the early church, God struck Ananias and Sapphira dead for lying about the price of a piece of property they sold. Paul warned the church at Corinth that because they had been guilty of sin as they celebrated the Lord's Supper, many of them were weak and sick, and a number had died (see 1 Cor. 11:29-30).

But a punishment for our sins can't be the only cause of suffering. This man was *born* blind. Could his parents then have been to blame?

Never has a generation lived that would accept this idea more readily than will ours. Thanks to Sigmund Freud, we're quick to look at any and all our problems and wail, "It was all Mom's fault!" In fact, our generation would, and does, accept this explanation without hesitation for most of our suffering. But is it correct? Scripture says that in a sense, it is, but not entirely.

When a pregnant woman abuses alcohol, chances are the child she carries will suffer brain damage. If a father abandons his family, his children are almost certain to suffer emotional upheaval leaving them with lifelong scars. Some of our suffering does come simply from living in a sinful world and having had sinful parents, though we're always free to choose our *response* to that suffering.

God holds *us* accountable for our response to the negative situations we encounter in life. That's the perspective Ezekial 18:4 teaches: "Every living soul belongs to Me, the father as well as the son—both alike belong to Me. *The soul who sins is the one who will die*" (italics added). At the same time, we know that when we sin, others are affected. I believe that's what the Lord refers to in Exodus 20:5. "I, the Lord your God, am a jealous God, punishing the children for the sin of the fathers to the third and fourth generation of those who hate Me."

The disciples tried to take the intricate mystery of why we suffer, boil it down to two choices, and force Jesus to check either (a) or (b). Job's friends made the same attempt. Job had lived a God-fearing life, winning praise from both man and God. Then trouble deluged him like an avalanche. Marauders stole his herds; fire from heaven destroyed his flocks; he lost his health, and worst of all, a freak accident snuffed out the lives of every one of his children. It's impossible to imagine deeper suffering. No wonder Job cursed the day he was born! But to Job's friends, the matter was clear-cut. Job suffered because of sin, so their challenge lay in uncovering what particular sin had brought on such monstrous maladies. When Job forsook his wrongdoing, all would again be well.

God did not agree with their easy diagnosis, just as Jesus didn't accept the disciples' assessment that sin must have caused the blind man's handicap. The suffering, Jesus explained, happened so the work of God could be displayed through this man's life.

It interests me that the disciples' first response to seeing the blind man was to wrangle over the "why" of his sightlessness. Already they had seen Jesus give sight to a number of the blind (Matt. 9:27-29; Mark 8:23-25). He had affirmed early in His ministry that healing the blind was one of the missions for which He was sent (Luke 4:18). With that information stored in their memories, why did they not, upon seeing this blind man, say, "Lord, there's a situation where You can honor Yourself! Will You help him, please?"

Instead, they decided to use this suffering as a case study to debate the correct theological reason for pain. But instead of a three-chapter discourse on the "why" of suffering, Jesus seemed more interested in looking at *how*—how God could be glorified through the man's situation.

I'm not suggesting we should never ask why when evil befalls us. The Prophet Habakkuk was revulsed at the Lord's revelation that the ruthless Chaldeans were going to conquer his people. So Habakkuk took his complaints to God, and then waited for the Lord's answer. From God's response to him, Habakkuk found the peace and strength he needed to rejoice in suffering. God *will* meet us in our pain, but He doesn't promise to open total understanding of all He is doing.

If we insist on knowing all the why's before we'll accept God's working, we may never find the comfort and help He longs to give. "Since the Lord is directing our steps, why try to understand everything that happens along the way?" (Prov. 20:24, TLB) Rather, we're wiser to respond as the Apostle Paul did when he suffered. He didn't understand all God's purposes, but of one thing he was certain: "I know whom I have believed, and am convinced that He is able to guard what I have entrusted to Him" (2 Tim. 1:12).

Suffering Can Provide an Arena to Glorify God

How can God's work be done through our suffering? The Scripture offers a number of possibilities.

Paul told the Corinthians that the misery he'd just been through was to remind him of *his need of God*. "We were under great pressure, far beyond our ability to endure, so that we despaired even of life. Indeed, in our hearts we felt the sentence of death. But this happened that we might not rely on ourselves but on God" (2 Cor. 1:8-9). Paul's pain produced the wonderful grace of dependence on God.

Sometimes God uses our suffering for the sake of *others*. Paul said, "If we are distressed, it is for your comfort and salvation" (2 Cor. 1:6). When you struggle, to whom do you go for encouragement and advice? You choose those who have been there, who have wrestled against the same problem. They have suffered for you, in a sense, so they can offer God's comfort to you in times of need.

Sometimes our pain comes simply because we belong to *Christ*, and the world hates us as they hate Him. Chuck lost his job because he refused to serve liquor to company customers he was responsible to entertain. Janice endures her family's ridicule because she has become a Christian and wants to follow the Lord. To sufferers like these, Peter wrote when he told the persecuted followers of Jesus to "rejoice that you participate in the sufferings of Christ, so that you may be overjoyed when His glory is revealed" (1 Peter 4:13).

There is also the suffering that comes as God's way of *maturing us*. He is the vinedresser who prunes away all that will keep us from the fruit-bearing lives we desire. But pruning hurts. The burning of His refining fire hurts. The whack of His shepherd's rod hurts. That's perhaps why Paul encouraged the Hebrews, "Endure hardship as a discipline; God is treating you as sons. Our fathers disciplined us for a little while as they thought best; but God disciplines us for our good, that we may share in His holiness. No discipline seems pleasant at the time, but painful. Later on, however, it produces a harvest of righteousness and peace for those who have been trained by it" (Heb. 12:7, 10-11).

Jesus said this man's blindness was allowed to provide a magnificent occasion for the manifestation of *God's glory*. Perhaps in the end that is the deepest and most abiding reason for all the pain we bear. This handicapped man was blind so Christ could show the power and love of the Heavenly Father to him, and to all those His life touched. God allowed this man's need, so He could have the pleasure of meeting it.

How we got to the point of suffering matters less than what we do once we're there. No matter why we suffer, our pain can always become a fertile seedbed in which the glory of God can take root and grow.

That is precisely what happened to this blind man. The Son of God gave him the gift of sight, used him to witness of the power of God to his family, his neighbors, and the Pharisees, and then brought him to clear and solid faith in Christ. God's power connected with this man's suffering, and all heaven broke loose! If, the day before he encountered Jesus, he had prayed, "God, thank You for this blindness, because it can give a wonderful opportunity for You to show Your goodness," he would have been right on target.

How do you deal with the pain you're currently feeling? Perhaps you're in pain because sometime or another you have prayed, "Lord, please show Your glory through my life," and He is doing that. We need to realize God intends to use our pain as a joy-filled opportunity to reveal Himself and His glory to us and through us. Any pain can be like this man's blindness, a showcase for the magnificence of God, if we so choose.

I'm not saying the choice will be easy. It wasn't for Candi when she was told she had cancer deep behind her sinuses. Doctors at the Mayo Clinic informed this beautiful young woman she faced a surgery in which they'd have to take out her eye, cut her skull open, and literally remove her face to get at the cancer. Candi survived the surgery, and the doctors put her back together as best they could, but her emotional pain in the aftermath of the "treatment" far exceeded her physical suffering. What could be the meaning of this terrible and seemingly senseless affliction?

But as she struggled, Candi turned to Christ for His strength, and during the year after the surgery she grew to know Him through Bible study and prayer. Candi didn't know how imperative her choice to accept God's help would be, for just a year later, she had to go through the same surgery *again*.

She agreed to the operation, but also told the Lord she wanted Him to be honored through her pain, and He has answered. During her hospitalization, Candi's peace was so obvious that many of the hospital personnel were touched. And since the operation, her illness has opened the door to a unique ministry. She's become a leader in the Alabama Junior Miss Pageant, because through the creative use of cosmetics, wigs, and scarves, she's still vibrantly attractive. But Candi tells the young women that beauty is fragile, and a relationship with Christ is life's only true stability. And they listen because His grace in her pain has made her living proof of the messages she shares.

We Can Trust God's Work Will Result in Our Good
When Jesus set out to heal this blind man, he spit on the ground, made a mud pack of the wet clay, and applied it to the man's eyes. This sounds like a concoction more likely to *cause* blindness than to cure it. The man may have thought himself worse off than before Jesus came

along. He did receive sight, but his healing put him at the center of a controversy that involved his neighbors, his family, and the local authorities. I don't know how this blind man felt about being a part of a big fight, but unless he was the kind to love a good scrap, all these happenings might have been highly uncomfortable for him.

When his neighbors demanded to know how it was he could now see, he simply told the truth. Yet these neighbors dragged him off to the Pharisees, who grilled him mercilessly about his healing. Again, he simply gave the facts, but when he did, it got him excommunicated from the synagogue, and consequently cut off from the entire religious structure he had grown up with. He didn't set out that day to offend his family, but even they turned their backs on him when they realized supporting his healing would mean excommunication for them too.

As he left the Pharisees' meeting hall, I wonder if this young man shook his head, stunned, and asked himself, "What happened here? All I did was receive sight from this man Jesus, and now I'm forsaken by everyone I've relied on. Did things get better, or did they actually get worse?"

As God helps us, things may seem to get worse before they get better. Scripture says this, "All things *work together* for good to them that love God" (Rom. 8:28, KJV, italics added). Though some things that happen along the way may seem to hold more pain than gain, we can be sure that when the entire mosaic is completed, God's design will bring overwhelming blessing to us. Jesus restored the blind man's sight, only to put him into a situation fraught with new difficulties. But the rejections and harrassment he endured after his healing prepared him for faith in the Messiah. He came to experience Christ not just as Healer, but as his Saviour from sin. Instead of mere physical sight, the blind man received a gift of far more worth: eternal life.

Bill is a 50-year-old, out-of-work farmer whose life, for the most part, has been a mess. Bill has been through two divorces, a mental breakdown, alcoholism, and financial disaster. But a few months ago, while watching a Billy Graham crusade on television, Bill decided to give himself to Christ. Did all the pain in his life immediately evaporate? Hardly. Less than a month after his decision, Bill flicked a match to light the pilot on his water heater and set off a gas explosion that destroyed his home and left him with burns over 70 percent of his body. Doctors gave Bill a 2-percent chance of even surviving.

Had the explosion occurred before Bill's spiritual renewal, we might have understood it. We would have agreed that those things just happen to people not living in God's favor. But Bill's life direction had just turned around. He looked to God for healing of his ruined life, and things got worse.

But did they?

Bill would say no. Even though he's still confined to the hospital, even though he's having to face painful skin grafting, even though a simple act like bathing his raw flesh causes him such pain that even through a haze of morphine he screams, Bill is doing well. He'll tell you the explosion happened for a purpose, and he believes God is bringing good from it. He survived the explosion by God's grace, and he trusts that with that same supernatural help, his future is going to be better than the past ever was. In the middle of a hospital burn unit, this ordinary man's life has become a temple from which the glory of God radiates.

Observable good is coming to Bill too. During the time he waivered between life and death, Bill was reconciled to his father and to two grown children from an early marriage he'd lost any hope of relating to. His wife has begun to grow spiritually, and the Lord has provided a home for them to replace the one destroyed in the explosion. Bill continues to heal remarkably, and his faith encourages those who come to encourage him.

To the short-sighted, it appears that God's healing may result in things getting worse instead of better. It seemed to happen that way for the blind man. But because we get to see the rest of his story, we know that's not accurate. After he was expelled from the synagogue, Jesus came and found him, and helped the now-sighted blind man to saving faith in Himself. And Christ allowed this man to know Him as few others did. To no one, except the Samaritan woman, did our Lord so frankly and so fully declare His own Messiahship. No one ever suffers for righteousness' sake without receiving great good from God.

Jesus touched this blind man, and the man came away not only seeing, but holding the gift of salvation. A whole new life was beginning for him. Let's allow his experience to encourage us to let God use our painful situations for His glory and our best good.

CHAPTER ELEVEN

Jesus and the Amazing Soldier

Though Jesus continually astounded those around Him, only twice in the Gospels was He put on record as being amazed Himself. In both instances, it was faith that caused Him to marvel. Mark tells us in his Gospel that the lack of faith shown by those in His hometown amazed the Lord. And Jesus was amazed by the faith of a troop commander in the Roman army.

I can think of no higher compliment than to have the Lord say that my faith made Jesus take notice! This army officer may have been an outsider to God's chosen house of Israel, but he obviously has some lessons to teach us about growing the kind of belief that pleases God.

When Jesus had finished saying all this in the hearing of the people, He entered Capernaum. There a centurion's servant, whom his master valued highly, was sick and about to die. The centurion heard of Jesus and sent some elders of the Jews to Him, asking Him to come and heal his servant. When they came to Jesus, they pleaded earnestly with Him,

"This man deserves to have You do this, because he loves our nation and has built our synagogue." So Jesus went with them.

He was not far from the house when the centurion sent friends to say to Him: "Lord, don't trouble Yourself, for I do not deserve to have You come under my roof. That is why I did not even consider myself worthy to come to You. But say the word, and my servant will be healed. For I myself am a man under authority, with soldiers under me. I tell this one, 'Go,' and he goes; and that one, 'Come,' and he comes. I say to my servant, 'Do this,' and he does it."

When Jesus heard this, He was amazed at him, and turning to the crowd following Him, He said, "I tell you, I have not found such great faith even in Israel." Then the men who had been sent returned to the house and found the servant well (Luke 7:1-10).

Three qualities mark this centurion's belief:
● He had a *loving faith*, one that cared for those he should have hated.
● He had a *humble faith*, one that admitted his unworthiness.
● He had a *solid faith*, founded on Christ's promises.

Faith in Jesus Results in Love

Most of the Romans regarded the Jews as little better than dogs, and they treated them accordingly. And *slaves* they considered property, nothing more. An estate management advisory of the day told farmers to annually take stock of their farming implements and their servants. Whatever was old or broken should be thrown away, man and machine alike.

This soldier was different; he loved the Jews. With his own money, he built them a place of worship. He loved his servant enough to seek out the best help he could find for the dying slave. True faith produces love.

Bob Boardman is another soldier who discovered such love taking root in him as he grew in genuine faith. During his service in World War II, Bob was shot in the neck by a Japanese sniper. Though he survived, his voice box was destroyed, leaving him able to communicate only in a husky whisper for the rest of his life. Yet after the war, Bob returned to Japan and spent the next thirty years communicating to his former enemies the good news of God's love.

The decision to return to Japan was not an easy one. Bob remembered, "Following Okinawa, the last battle of the war, God clearly showed me that I was to follow Him somewhere overseas to serve Him. But going to Japan never entered my thoughts. When the call became clear that it was to be the land of my former enemy, I was shocked. I could not accept such a fate. Impossible and unreasonable! For almost two months I struggled with God. I was firmly against going to Japan." But Bob did at last submit to God's direction, and during his service there saw the Lord give such love and respect for the Japanese that he would say, "Over a period of many years, my wartime enemies have become my best friends."[1]

Faith without works is a dead faith, the Apostle James firmly asserts. He would have cheered at the reality of the centurion's belief, because the soldier rolled up his sleeves and went to work, serving those he should have detested. True faith generates good works motivated by love for those we couldn't have loved before.

Jesus admonished His followers, "You have heard that it was said, 'Love your neighbor and hate your enemy.'

But I tell you: Love your enemies and pray for those who persecute you, that you may be sons of your Father in heaven" (Matt. 5:43-45). The genuineness of your faith won't be shown so much by the flashy deeds that it does, as by how much love it generates. Love for our enemies is the truest barometer of our faith. By this barometer, the Roman centurion could predict clear and sunny days of growth ahead, because he loved those he should have hated.

A Humble Faith Understands Our Unworthiness before God
Was the centurion worthy of Christ's help or not? The Jews who came to Jesus on his behalf insisted that he was highly deserving, and they backed up their claims with proofs of the soldier's generosity and caring. Compared to other Roman soldiers, this man was certainly worthy.

But the centurion had a different idea. His message to Christ was, "I do not deserve to have You come under my roof. That is why I did not even consider myself worthy to come to You." This soldier didn't compare himself to other men. He used Christ's life as his standard, and next to the Saviour, he knew he couldn't measure up. Everything has to do with what you're comparing to.

Chuck Swindoll tells the story of a college girl who faced the unhappy prospect of telling her parents about some bad grades and her need for more money. But when she wrote them, she used the comparison principle to her distinct advantage. She wrote,

"Dear Mom and Dad,

Just thought I'd drop you a note to clue you in on my plans. I have fallen in love with a guy named Jim. He quit high school after grade eleven to get married. About a year ago he got divorced. We've been going steady for two months and plan to be married in the fall. Until then I've decided to move into his apartment. I think I might be pregnant. At any rate, I dropped out of school last week, although I would like to finish college sometime in the future."

On the next page she added,

"Mom and Dad, I just want you to know that everything I've written so far in this letter is false. None of it is true, but it is true that I got a C- in French and flunked Math. It is true that I am going to need some more money for my tuition payments."[2]

How bad things are depend on your basis of comparison. And how worthy we are depends on who we are compared to.

When the encyclopedia lists epidemics that ran rampant through societies, the entries include things like smallpox, diptheria, malaria, and the bubonic plague. But when the encyclopedia for the year 2001 is released, it's likely to have added a new plague to the list, one that has infected most of our society during the last half of the twentieth century. That affliction is low self-esteem.

We're well aware of the negative effects of low self-esteem. According to popular literature, it generates child and spouse abuse, chemical dependency, crime, divorce, job failure, overweight, scholastic underachievement, and myriad other maladies. Everyone seems to have at least a touch of it, yet no one seems clear on how exactly to cure it. We consider it such a crippler, it's easy to feel we can't have low self-esteem and still be pleasing to God.

But Jesus' care for this humble centurion shows clearly how false that idea is! Rather than a guaranteed hindrance to faith, sometimes what looks like low self-esteem might actually be a wonderful sense of holy unworthiness that convinces us how much we need God's help.

"Love others as you love yourself!" This scriptural admonition is certainly true, but I sometimes fear we make too much of measuring how much we love ourselves. Christ doesn't help us because we feel deserving; He helps us because He is loving and gracious and kind. In fact, a healthy dose of unworthiness could be highly beneficial for our spiritual lives. Jesus said, "Blessed are the poor in spirit, for theirs is the kingdom of heaven" (Matt. 5:3).

A young man I know told me, "I've found out something. You've got to get lost before you can be saved. I am good and lost now. I know that I am unworthy. I never realized that I was ruined, that I could never earn God's acceptance. Now I am ready to commit my life to Jesus Christ."

In a thought-provoking article entitled "The Blessings of Mental Anguish," philosophy professor Stephen Evans offers encouragement to those of us who often question our potential for usefulness to God. "All of us can probably think of Christians who were a little 'odd,' and were able to do great things for God in part because of their oddness." He cites the example of the famous preacher Charles Spurgeon. Spurgeon was frequently confined to bed for weeks at a time by his psychological and physical illnesses. Prolonged bouts of depression often plagued him. Yet he published over 3,500 sermons and wrote 135 books. Many regarded him as the outstanding preacher of his generation. Spurgeon was able to achieve such accomplishments in spite of his depression as he came to see his problems as part of God's work in his life. He allowed them to make him more sensitive to others in pain. He observed that an unusual spiritual blessing often followed periods of great psychological suffering, so he began to see the depression as a herald of a new work of God beginning, instead of as an enemy.[3]

Vernon C. Grounds, head of the Grounds Counseling Center in Denver, would applaud Spurgeon's perspective. He reflects, "An individual, quite completely free from tension, anxiety, and conflict, may be only a well-adjusted sinner who is dangerously maladjusted to God; and it is infinitely better to be a neurotic saint than a healthy-minded sinner."[4]

If you struggle with low self-esteem, work at seeing the value you have to God. At the same time, don't let your lack of self-esteem keep you from believing Christ. Feelings, after all, are only feelings. They certainly don't constitute the substance of what makes up our faith. Faith can thrive deep, solid, and healthy at the core of your being, even though on the level of your emotions you may *feel* as full of faith as a cup with the bottom knocked out is full of water. Faith isn't feeling confident; it's acting in light of what you know is true, whether you feel like it or not. Remember that this centurion didn't need swaggering self-confidence to care passionately about his ailing servant, and to exhibit trust that amazed Christ. He needed only the good sense to accept help from the Right Source.

Faith in Jesus Grows as We Know His Promises

From this Roman soldier we hear one of the strongest statements of unadulterated belief recorded in the New Testament (see Luke 7:6-8). He said, "Lord, You don't even need to come here to heal him—just speak, and he'll be well. My servants respond to my authority; just as surely this illness will submit to your command." The soldier could believe solidly, because he heard Christ's promise to help and accepted the authority of His word.

When Jesus heard about the ailing servant, Matthew records He said, "I will go and heal him" (Matt. 8:7). Later, He gave the centurion this specific assurance, "It will be done just as you believed it would" (Matt. 8:13). The centurion could have such strong faith because he had received such solid promises from Christ. When our faith is founded on the Word of God, it can be confident faith, indeed.

Not everyone tries to build faith on such a solid foundation. Some of us feel like the little boy in Sunday School who said, "Faith is believing things you know are not true!" If falsehoods are the basis of our faith, we're sure to be scuttled. Yet Christianity isn't built on falsehoods; it's based on eternal truth.

We often talk of faith to believe the impossible. Is that what we're to trust? If we are, we'd take our guidance on how to do it from the Wicked Queen in the children's tale *Alice in Wonderland*.

The Queen tells Alice, "I'll give you something to believe. I am a hundred and one, five months and a day. Can you believe that?"

Alice said, "I can't believe that."

The Queen says in a pitying tone, "Try again. Draw a long breath and shut your eyes."

Alice laughed. "There's no use trying. I can't believe impossible things."

The Queen says, "You can't? You probably haven't had much practice. When I was your age, I always practiced a half-an-hour a day believing impossible things. I believed as many as six impossible things before breakfast."[5]

No, growing in the Christian faith doesn't mean trying to believe six impossible things before breakfast, because just as our faith isn't built on falsehoods, it isn't built on the impossible. The foundation of our faith is the *promise* of One who does not lie. We found our faith on the Word of God, just as the centurion did. We don't rest on wishful thinking or delirious desires, but on what God has said. That's Paul's emphasis when he writes: "*Faith* comes from hearing the message, and the message is heard through the *Word of Christ*" (Rom. 10:17, italics added). This Word we can stake our lives on, and follow, and obey. It's given to us plainly in the Bible and made alive to us by the living Christ who dwells within us.

A scriptural illustration may help us understand how hearing the Word of Christ can energize our faith.

Luke 5 records the story of calling of the first disciples. Jesus had been out in Simon's boat on Lake Gennesaret, preaching to the people on shore. When He finished, He told Simon to sail out into the deep water, and net himself a catch of fish. Simon protested. "Master, we've worked hard all night and haven't caught anything."

But Simon had something solid in which to believe. He had the Lord's promise that this time throwing his net into the lake would produce a catch. So Simon responded in faith, and said, "Because You say so, I will let down the nets."

What happened? They caught so many fish that their nets began to break! They even had to call for a second boat to help, and the catch filled both vessels so full they began to sink.

Now, since the start of history, godly people have gone fishing. They did it centuries before Simon, and have continued since. But every time one of God's people throws a baited hook in the water, an 18-pound bass doesn't grab onto the line. (I can attest to this by personal experience!) But Simon brought home a record catch because he had a promise from Christ, and he showed faith in that promise by going fishing.

How can we grow in believing God's promises? Matthew 7:7 gives us Christ's answer to this question. "Ask and it will be given to you; seek and you will find; knock and the door will be opened to you."

First and most important, we need to *ask for His help*. The centurion sought Christ's aid. Of course, Simon's successful catch of fish illustrates the fact that sometimes

Christ reminds us of wonderful promises even without our asking. But if He doesn't, we need to ask Him what He wants to do about our particular situation.

Second, we need to *seek* God. Seek means to go after God, to determine to persist after Him until He makes His Word known. As we wait, God's Spirit will often confirm His Word to us by settling an unshakeable peace inside us that He wants to move in a certain direction on our behalf.

This seeking phase may take some time. For some years our church was strangled by inadequate parking facilities, but since we were landlocked, there seemed to be no easy answer. The church officers asked the Lord to direct us, but it was ten years before His answer came clear to us. In the meantime, nothing opened up, and we couldn't even agree on what direction we should go.

A ten-year wait added up to over five hundred Sunday mornings we struggled with parking, but we determined to act only on God's direction. When He did begin to move, it was like the tumblers on a lock clicking into place. Land became available, the officers agreed unanimously on a course of action, and the congregation overwhelmingly supported the plan. How glad we were we had continued to seek until God gave His answer.

Third, we need to *knock*, encourage our faith by an action in light of what God has said He wants to do. When Jesus said He would heal the ailing servant, the centurion took action by faith. He told Christ to not even bother to come because a simple word from One with such authority would be more than sufficient to raise the dying man. Notice that the centurion's response to Christ had to do with *how* Christ would accomplish the healing, not whether or not the healing would take place. His faith was settled, and he acted in light of it.

Simon acted on Christ's promise when he set sail to the

middle of the lake. Moses acted on God's promise when he stepped into the Red Sea. Noah acted on God's promise when he began cutting timber to build the ark. Without God's promise, each of these acts would have been foolish at best. But when Christ's promise is mixed with faith, God's work goes forward.

Does the centurion's kind of faith sound unattainable? Too mystical? Too extravagant? If it does, you may be encouraged to remember that Roman centurions were not, on the whole, a flamboyant lot. Like the master sergeants in today's army, they were the nuts-and-bolts people who quietly kept the Roman military machinery moving. One historian decribed them as sturdy and steady soldiers who didn't rush into danger but didn't run from it either. Yet it was this kind of common sense, meat-and-potatoes sort of person who demonstrated such remarkable and electric faith in Jesus.

Exercising faith doesn't mean you have to be dynamically daring, or aggravatingly aggressive, or a rash risktaker by nature. Our centurion makes it clear that anyone can see Christ work for him or her, as long as faith accepts what God says as true and acts on it in love.

NOTES

1. Bob Boardman, *A Higher Honor* (Colorado Springs, Colorado: Navpress, 1987), pp. 15-16.

2. Charles R. Swindoll, *Growing Strong in the Seasons of Life* (Portland, Oregon: Multnomah Press, 1983), pp. 71-73.

3. C. Stephen Evans, "The Blessings of Mental Anguish," in *Christianity Today*, January 17, 1986, pp. 27, 29.

4. Vernon C. Grounds, "Called to Be Saints—Not Well-Adjusted Sinners," in *Christianity Today*, January 17, 1986, p. 28.

5. Lewis Carroll, *Through the Looking Glass* (New York: Grosset and Dunlap, Inc.), 1946.

CHAPTER TWELVE

Jesus and the Theologian

Do you like riddles? Here's one I'm sure you won't solve quickly. What do a newborn baby, a gusty breeze, and a snake wrapped around a pole have in common? Give up? The answer is found in the third chapter of John's Gospel. All three are illustrations Jesus used as He explained eternal life to a noted theologian. As we investigate these word pictures our Lord chose, I trust you'll understand more clearly what life with God means and how we can be part of it.

Now there was a man of the Pharisees named Nicodemus, a member of the Jewish ruling council. He came to Jesus at night and said, "Rabbi, we know You are a teacher who has come from God. For no one could perform the miraculous signs You are doing if God were not with him."
In reply Jesus declared, "I tell you the truth, unless a man is born again, he cannot see the kingdom of God."
"How can a man be born when he is old?"

Nicodemus asked. "Surely he cannot enter a second time into his mother's womb to be born!"

Jesus answered, "I tell you the truth, unless a man is born of water and the Spirit, he cannot enter the kingdom of God. Flesh gives birth to flesh, but the Spirit gives birth to spirit. You should not be surprised at My saying, 'You must be born again.' The wind blows wherever it pleases. You hear its sound, but you cannot tell where it comes from or where it is going. So it is with everyone born of the Spirit.

"Just as Moses lifted up the snake in the desert, so the Son of Man must be lifted up, that everyone who believes in Him may have eternal life.

"For God so loved the world that He gave His one and only Son, that whoever believes in Him shall not perish but have eternal life" (John 3:1-8, 14-16).

Spiritual Life Starts with a Spiritual Birth

"Unless a man is born again," Jesus told Nicodemus, "he cannot see the kingdom of God."

Perhaps Jesus knew Nicodemus was curious about the kingdom of God. God's kingship over Israel was a theme all Jews knew well, but John the Baptist had renewed people's interest in the subject as he preached the kingdom was near. When people asked John the Baptist what to do to save themselves from the coming wrath, he talked about repentance and bringing forth fruit worthy of repentance, such as sharing what they had with those who lacked, being honest in their business dealings, being content with their pay, and being baptized in the Jordan River.

A God-seeking Jew like Nicodemus must have praised John's efforts. John's methods were unorthodox, and baptism offered a new wrinkle on old themes, but John moved the people to right behavior. Nicodemus saw keeping the externals in line as the way to find God's favor, so he felt little conflict between what John preached and what Jews who loved God practiced. So when Nicodemus sought out Jesus, he was confounded when Jesus told him that the kingdom of God belonged only to those who have been born a second time.

Actually, this pronouncement shouldn't have mystified Nicodemus. His life's work consisted of knowing the Scriptures, and this new birth is taught in the Old Testament. The Sovereign Lord says to Israel, "I will sprinkle clean water on you, and you will be clean; I will cleanse you from all your impurities and from all your idols. I will give you a new heart and put a new spirit in you; I will remove from you your heart of stone and give you a heart of flesh" (Ezek. 36:25-26). And earlier, God promised the time would come when "I will put My law in their minds and write it on their hearts. I will be their God and they will be My people" (Jer. 31:33). He's saying, "I will do a deep work in your inner nature that will change your life and cleanse you." That is the new birth.

Jack Eckerd was a 69-year-old business executive who had heard the claims of Christ, but struggled with accepting them. "After all, I had been running my own life for most of 69 years," Jack explained later. But Chuck Colson challenged his ambivalence. "I can't understand you business executives who are used to making major decisions. Then along comes the most important decision you will ever make, and you equivocate. You sit on the fence." Jack realized Colson was right in calling him to task, and he surrendered to the Lord.

Now, Jack says, he "lives under a new table of organization, with Jesus Christ as Chairman of the Board and Chief Executive Officer." His new CEO has called for some changes, as He directed Jack to persuade the new president of Eckerd's Drugs to remove all obscene material from their 1,200 stores. But in these changes, and many others, Jack rejoices. He claims he understands why Jesus would call this experience being born again, because Jack says he feels like a new man![1]

Nicodemus didn't grasp what this new birth meant, so Jesus tried a fuller explanation. "Unless a man is born of water and the Spirit," He said, "he cannot enter the kingdom of God."

People differ in what they think Jesus refers to when He speaks of the need to be "born of water" to enter the kingdom. Some think He meant we won't be able to enter heaven unless we've been baptized, but the rest of the New Testament doesn't bear this teaching out. Paul said, "Christ did not send me to baptize, but to preach the Gospel" (1 Cor. 1:17). If baptism had been necessary for salvation, surely this great messenger of the Gospel would have led his followers to experience all they needed for salvation. But Paul understood that baptism only testifies of conversion; it doesn't create it.

Others think Jesus meant we need to repent of our sins to enter God's kingdom when He said we must be "born of water."[2] Still others say the need to be born of water points to the Word as God's instrument purifying us.[3]

I think when Jesus said we needed to be born of water, He was talking about our physical birth. In physical birth, we are carried for nine months in amniotic fluid and are born out of water. Physical birth is a necessity to be living on earth in the flesh. In the same way, spiritual birth is required if we are to have life in the Spirit. We need our spirits quickened, our souls made alive by God.

Birthed once, then birthed again. No wonder Nicodemus shook his head at Jesus' statement. Until that moment, Nicodemus has believed that keeping God's Law would gain him eternal life and a place in God's kingdom. Though keeping the Law was by no means easy, in his view, it was accomplishable. But this—this new birth—was obviously impossible by any means known to man. And that, of course, was the Lord's point. The only way to be a part of God's life is a way utterly impossible to accomplish by human effort.

John Wesley put it this way:

Be you baptized or unbaptized, "you must be born again"; otherwise it is not possible you should be inwardly holy: and without inward as well as outward holiness, you cannot be happy, even in this world, much less in the world to come.

Do you say, "Nay, but I do no harm to any man; I am honest and just in all my dealings; I do not curse, or take the Lord's name in vain; I do not profane the Lord's day; I am no drunkard; I do not slander my neighbour, nor live in any wilful sin"? If this be so, it were much to be wished that all men went as far as you do. But you must go farther yet, or you cannot be saved: still, "you must be born again."

Do you add, "I do go farther yet; for I not only do no harm, but do all the good I can"? I doubt that fact; I fear you have had a thousand opportunities of doing good which you have suffered to pass by unimproved, and for which therefore you are accountable to God. But if you had improved them all, if you really had done all the good you possibly could to all men, yet this does not at all alter the case; still "you must be born again." Without this, nothing will do any good to your poor, sinful, polluted soul.

"Nay, but I constantly attend all the ordinances of God: keep to my church and sacrament." It is well you do: but all this will not keep you from hell, except you be born again. Go to church twice a day; go to the Lord's table every week; say ever so many prayers in private; hear ever so many good sermons; read ever so many good books; still "you must be born again."[1]

Do you get the idea Wesley believed Jesus meant what He said when He insisted we be born again? Perhaps he beat this drum so insistently and repeatedly because we have such a difficult time grasping this truth. Nicodemus certainly did, and he was a teacher of religion.

Nicodemus knew how to please God. The Lord Himself had carved it in the stone of the Ten Commandments and embellished on those orders in the Old Testament Law. Imagine the shake-up to Nicodemus' belief system when Jesus told him that attaining eternal life was not through keeping rules. Asking Nicodemus to make such a violent turnaround in belief would be like radioing Mario Andretti when he's headed for the Indy finish line and asking him to throw his car into reverse. Can you imagine the mass of smoking gears under that car's chassis after he did? Yet Jesus asked Nicodemus to throw his belief system into reverse, even though it may have meant stripping every religious gear upon which he had depended. But without a totally new life, entering the kingdom of God simply isn't possible.

To Be Born Again, God Has to Reach Down to Us
Connecting with God is like being blown on by the wind, Jesus explained, and He points out three truths about gusty gales so Nicodemus might understand.

First, the wind blows wherever it pleases; you don't tell the wind what to do. If you don't believe me, talk with people who live in tornado zones or hurricane-prone parts of the country. We've begun to conquer outer space, but when the radio blares tornado warnings, we're forced to run for cover, just as people have for centuries before us. Like the wind, so is the new birth controlled only by God. All our efforts to win it accomplish nothing.

Second, the wind is mysterious. We hear its roar, but we can't tell where it's coming from or where it will go next. So it is with life from God. The great mystery writer Agatha Christie might have been intrigued by the New Testament, because Scripture is filled with mysteries. It speaks of the mystery of the Gospel, of faith, of godliness, of the kingdom, even of God Himself. The Resurrection is a mystery, as is the way marriages create a picture of Christ and His church. We can know and be part of all these truths, but we can't explain them. They will continue to be mysterious until we know all completely in heaven. Accepting a faith that makes room for mystery isn't easy for some of us. Perhaps it wasn't for Nicodemus, who had invested his life in eliminating mystery.

The Pharisees had their mysteries solved. Words like ambiguity, nuance, uncertainty, and vagueness could be deleted from their vocabularies altogether. Why keep words you're never going to need? The point of their lives was to keep the Law, and the Law covered every point of their lives. They had truth hermetically sealed; the journey to find answers had ended. God had been neatly and inescapably boxed. But the Greek words for "wind" and "Spirit" come from the same root, and like the wind, God's Spirit can't be enclosed.

Third, the wind has effects. When the wind blows you over, you know it. No meteorologist has to present you with a heap of statistics and laws of physics to convince you the wind has power if it has just demolished your house. So it is with God's life. You needn't be able to explain all He does to have His power transform you.

A salesman I know saw his life turned around by the powerful wind of God's life. We met when a mutual friend initiated a conversation between us about Christ. This salesman understood the Gospel for the first time the night we talked, but he feared giving his life to Christ, because he knew it might cost him his job. His boss had him giving kickbacks to purchasing agents. The salesman knew the kickbacks were wrong, since they had to be handled "under the table." Turning to Christ would mean turning from this sin. But he was in no position to lose his job. He and his wife had just moved into a lovely new home, were making payments on a car, had several of their children enrolled in private school, and had a new baby. Coming to Christ might mean losing all this.

The salesman chose Christ. When he told his boss he could no longer be a part of the kickbacks, his boss said, "You're going to have to do it. If not, I'm going to have to let you go. Which way do you want it?" But the salesman's decision had already been made, and he lost his job.

He went three months without a job. He lost one car and had to take his children out of the private school. These weren't easy trials for a newly born Christian. But he'll tell you his life in Christ is the greatest thing that ever happened to him and his family. His spiritual growth has been apparent and steady, and he now carries a leadership role in our church. He's also hard at work at a new job, managing a business for another Christian.

God's life arrives like the wind, blowing where it wants to, and leaving changed lives in its wake. As mysteriously as the wind, God reaches down to us, and the stage is set for the new birth.

In the Outworking of the New Birth, We Reach up to God
"Just as Moses lifted up the snake in the desert, so the Son of Man must be lifted up, that everyone who believes in Him may have eternal life" (John 3:14).

This time the noted teacher of Israel's history could have no excuse for not understanding, because the story Jesus used to illustrate new life came straight from the pages of the Old Testament.

The incident Jesus refers to is recorded in Numbers 21. During their wanderings in the wilderness, the Israelites had plenty of time to complain, and they exercised their option at every chance, it seemed. This time they grumbled over the food and water the Lord provided. So God sent poisonous snakes among them, and many died from snakebite. When the people repented of their ungratefulness, Moses prayed for them, and the Lord responded in a most unusual way.

"The Lord said to Moses, 'Make a snake and put it up on a pole; anyone who is bitten can look at it and live.' So Moses made a bronze snake and put it up on a pole. Then when anyone was bitten by a snake and looked at the bronze snake, he lived" (Num. 21:8-9).

All they needed was to look at the snake, and they lived. But even though the way to life was simple enough for a child to follow, there surely were those of Israel's camp who refused it. Suppose an Israelite crawls into his tent, half-dead from the effects of a snakebite. As he waits to die, his wife rushes into the tent. "Honey! I have the most wonderful news! God has given Moses a cure for these snakebites! God told him to make a snake and lift it high on a pole. If we just look at it, we don't have to die. Come on out and save yourself."

But he just laughs. "Look at a bronze snake on a pole and be saved from death? That's the most ridiculous thing I ever heard of. I'm not going to give in to that kind of foolishness."

That man would have died, though life awaited just outside the door of his tent.

Centuries later, the Son of God would be lifted up on a

cross, so humanity could be saved from eternal death simply by looking to Him in faith. What a picture of redemption that bronze snake would provide! Do you wonder why God would use a snake to symbolize His holy Son, since in Scripture, a snake is associated with evil? The reason is clear. God would take His Son, who knew no sin, and "make Him to be sin for us." All our evil fell to Christ; all our sin was laid on Him, so we could find salvation by looking in faith at this Son made a snake, raised up on a pole.

Though Gestation Takes Time, Birth Finally Comes

New life begins as God's Spirit reaches down, and our belief then reaches up as a new creature in Christ is born. But birth may not come the first day the message is presented. It didn't for Nicodemus.

Nicodemus began his initiative toward Jesus cautiously, coming to meet Him under the cover of night. John doesn't tell us what transpired that night in Nicodemus' heart, but this meeting with Jesus must have left him shaken and wondering.

Nicodemus is mentioned two other times in Scripture. In John 7, Jesus preached in Jerusalem at the Feast of the Tabernacles. When many in the crowd put their trust in Him, the Pharisees decided He could not continue, and sent temple guards to arrest Him. But the guards came back empty-handed. Because Jesus spoke with such authority, the guards simply could not bring themselves to arrest Him. Naturally, the Pharisees raged. As proof of His unworthiness, they sneered that only the ignorant believed in Him—no one of any learning or religious status had taken such a step.

In their midst stood Nicodemus, and he spoke on Jesus' behalf, but caution still controlled him. He did not say he believed Jesus to be the Messiah, nor did he offer a ringing defense of Christ. He'd apparently told no one of his meeting with Jesus, because the other Pharisees seemed not to know any of their number showed an interest in Jesus. But he appeared to be journeying toward faith, because he did ask, "Does our law condemn a man without hearing him out?"

Perhaps Nicodemus thought that if the other Pharisees would actually talk to Jesus, and listen to what He had to say as Nicodemus himself had done, they might consider His claims also. If some did, then Nicodemus would have support from others in his group for his emerging faith. But the other Pharisees disdained him. "Don't you know the Messiah can't come from Galilee?" Nicodemus said no more. He had spoken up cautiously, but he did speak. There is an intimation the seed of faith was beginning to grow.

But after Jesus' death, the Scriptures record a clear indication of faith flowering in this Pharisee. When all the Lord's disciples fled, two men stepped forward to ask Pilate for Christ's body—Joseph of Arimethea . . . and Nicodemus.

Perhaps it wasn't until Nicodemus saw Jesus on the cross that he understood the serpent on the pole Jesus had spoken of. Jesus Himself would become the serpent, provided by God to cure the ills of the world. "God so loved the world that He gave His one and only Son." The words beat themselves into Nicodemus' brain as he thought of the bleeding figure agonizing on the cross. *This* was the Son, sent from God! "Whoever *believes* in Him shall not perish but have eternal life." Human effort meant nothing at all. This Man on the cross was the way to life! Nicodemus gladly received God's provision for eternal life, as at that moment, a spiritual infant gasped for his first chestful of air as the noted theologian was born again.

Have you been born again? Or like this God-fearing religious leader, have you been trying to earn your way into God's life by trying hard to be good enough? Right now could be your moment of birth. John 3:16 is the 26-word fulcrum on which all of humanity's destiny balances. By choosing to put our trust in Christ, we can tip the balance of our futures to God's side, and with Him we will live for all eternity.

NOTES

1. Jack Eckerd, "Change of Command," *Guideposts*, August 1986, p. 16.

2. As John baptized, he preached repentance for the forgiveness of sins (Mark 1:4).

3. Ephesians 5:25-26 teaches, "Christ loved the church and gave Himself up for her to make her holy, cleansing her by the *washing with water* through *the word*" (italics added).

4. John Wesley, *The New Birth* (London: Crusade Publishers, 1963), p. 11.